lemons

lemons
growing, cooking, crafting

By **Kate Chynoweth** and **Elizabeth Woodson**

Photographs by **Rita Maas**

CHRONICLE BOOKS

SAN FRANCISCO

Library of Congress Cataloging-in-Publication Data available.
ISBN: 0-8118-3713-0
Manufactured in Hong Kong

Text by Kate Chynoweth
Recipes and recipe text by Elizabeth Woodson
Prop styling by Barbara Fritz
Food styling by Megan Fawn Schlow
Designed and illustrated by Azi Rad
Typeset by Kristen Wurz

Distributed in Canada by Raincoast Books
9050 Shaughnessy Street
Vancouver, British Columbia V6P 6E5

10 9 8 7 6 5 4 3 2 1

Chronicle Books LLC
85 Second Street
San Francisco, California 94105

www.chroniclebooks.com

acknowledgments

We would like to thank Mikyla Bruder, our editor, for her clear vision and
constant support, as well as Jodi Davis of Chronicle Books, and copy
editor Sharilyn Hovind. Also, thanks to Dave Griffith, and the friends
whose knowledge of food and food history became an invaluable resource:
Sarah Putman Clegg, Emily Miller, Christina Henry, and Richard Wilson.
And to dinner-party guests and advice givers Irene and Lynn Woodson,
Tina Ujlaki, Richard Marmet, Susanne and Chris Davis, Danielle and
James Menk, and Susan Herr, and "Sweet Treats" recipe tasters Nicholas,
Chloe, Hadley, and George. Special appreciation goes to Rita Maas for
translating our words into art with her lovely photography.

contents

introduction

With its delicious scent, appealing sour flavor, vivid yellow color, and powerfully acidic juice, the lemon offers many practical benefits and seductive charms. Lemons are perhaps most appreciated in the kitchen, and the fruit's rich culinary history shows it to be a beloved staple around the world. In the sixteenth century, the Italians first paired lemon and fish, while Victorian cooks created transparent puddings to show off bright morsels of zest. The French invented lemonade as we know it today, and in Sicily, a traditional snack of lemon slices dipped in cayenne pepper and salt still makes intrepid culinary explorers pucker up.

The lemon is equally admired outside the realm of cookery. In the gardens of antiquity, the tree became a status symbol, cultivated for its glossy leaves and pearly, sweet-scented blossoms rather than its fruit, and eventually flourished as a decorative element in Renaissance gardens as well. The medical uses of the lemon have made history, too. Hundreds of years ago, Indian doctors used the fruit to cure an enlarged spleen, while the British Royal Navy prevented sailors from dying of scurvy by providing rations of the vitamin C–laden juice. Today, lemons are still revered for their tonic effects. Some doctors advise patients to bite into lemon slices to fight off nausea, while citrus enthusiasts drink the juice of one fruit in water every morning for their digestive health. Even in their most practical incarnations, such as scented household cleansers and candles, lemons freshen and purify.

In this book, you'll find classic recipes and crafts alongside fresh and innovative ways to appreciate lemons. If you enjoy delicious lemony dishes, try a creamy lemon curd, or an easy Italian *gremolata* to bring tangy flavor to grilled fish or roasted meat. If you'd like to try cultivating your own fresh lemons, you can learn how best to coax fruit from your trees or (if you're in a colder climate) to find the right variety for indoor growing. If handmade potions and crafts are more your style, spend an afternoon with friends making scented holiday pomanders or luxurious beauty treats like lemon creamsicle soap.

Whether you share the creative ideas and favorite dishes in these pages with loved ones, or experiment and adapt them to your own tastes, finding the time to appreciate lemons will bring many rewards. Since ancient times, the lemon has sparked human imaginations—starting today, let it light up your own.

lemon lore

fascinating facts and ancient history

Prized for its natural beauty and refreshing flavor, the fruit of the *Citrus limon* tree originated in northwest India over two thousand years ago. Over centuries of cultivation, the lemon spread from ancient India to North Africa, Spain, and the New World, eventually transforming from an exotic, rare fruit to an essential staple of the common kitchen. The lemon tree itself, boasting glossy green foliage and aromatic white blossoms, ranks among the most classic elements of garden design. Packed with vitamin C, a powerful anti-oxidant, the lemon has potent medicinal qualities, and its juice provided the first known prevention for scurvy, long the scourge of seamen. Perhaps the most delightful aspect of the lemon comes in the simple culinary feats it performs in the kitchen. The piquant juice and delicious zest complement sweet and savory dishes equally well, and a bowl of ripe golden lemons is an essential component of the well-stocked kitchen. Today lemons are grown on nearly every continent, and for cooks around the world, their tart flavor is nearly as essential as salt.

The history of the lemon can be traced back to the moment it reached the Mediterranean, although opinions diverge on the exact date. An early theory suggests that the lemon tree spread through the region as late as the tenth century. Today, the more widely accepted view is that Romans brought the fruit westward thousands of years before, around A.D. 100, when they began trading with India. Although written evidence of successful lemon cultivation in Rome does not exist, ancient art from the first century suggests that they were part of the landscape. What some experts regard indisputably as lemons appear in the frescoes of Pompeii and mosaic pavement found in Tusculum (now Frascati). Since then, lemons have remained a favorite subject with artists, and the golden fruit appears everywhere, from luminous Renaissance paintings to the bright, modern works of Braque and Matisse.

In ancient India, lemons flavored both food and drink, particularly an alcoholic punch that combined the tart juice with spirits—but the Romans did not acquire a taste for the fruit from their early encounters. They regarded lemons as curiosities and decorations, and used vinegar to sharpen food rather than citrus. Indeed, a Latin word for "lemon" did not exist. Considering how little practical use Rome derived from the fruit, it is not surprising that after the fall of the empire, lemons fell by the wayside. Besides, it seems only fitting that as the Dark Ages later gripped Europe, the bright sunny fruit was nowhere to be found.

The lemon returned to the Mediterranean during the Arab expansion, starting in the fourth century. Arabs had discovered the lemon after conquering the Middle East, and like their Persian predecessors, used the sharp, tangy citrus fruit to improve the taste of fatty mutton. Arab cooks, who strongly flavored foods with spices and salt, eventually incorporated the pungent lemon into all sorts of dishes. After extending their control to the coast of northern Africa, Arabs (known as Moors) conquered the Visigothic kingdom of Spain. Everywhere they went, the lemon soon followed. Arabs also spread lemons to China. The first written records of the fruit appear during the Sung dynasty (A.D. 960–1279), and the Chinese name *li mung* is considered an imported derivation.

Lemons remained relatively rare during the Middle Ages and were used only by the wealthy. Over subsequent centuries, however, they flourished and spread to North Africa and throughout the Mediterranean. Lemons particularly thrived in sun-drenched Morocco, Tunisia, and Algeria, where they became integral to the cultures and cuisines. A chief ingredient in the *harira* soup that North Africans use to break the fast of Ramadan, fresh lemon juice also contributes tartness to rich sauces for stuffed vegetable dishes and garnishes

makhouda, the savory, crustless quiche that resembles Italian frittata. Preserved lemons, or *l'hamd mrakad,* another hallmark of Moroccan cuisine, add a salty and tangy flavor to traditional stews, or *tagines.* The sunny Mediterranean climate produces bountiful lemon harvests, and the plentiful tart ingredient has inspired many culinary classics, such as the rich lemony Greek soup *avgolemono* and the flavorful sauce for fried fish that goes by the same name. Today, as in the past, the refreshing taste of the lemon remains one of the distinctive and delightful flavors of the Mediterranean table.

preserved lemons

Preserved lemons have a lengthy and fascinating history. The thirteenth-century Syrian cookbook *Kitâb al-Wusla ila al-Habîb,* translated as *The Link to the Beloved,* includes an entire section on "salty lemons," which, the book states, are "so well known, they need no description." Some form of preserved and pickled lemons appear in the cuisines of the region that stretches from India to North Africa, including Afghanistan, Pakistan, Syria, and Egypt. In most recipes, lemons are pickled in their own juice (vinegar is sometimes substituted). In Morocco, pickled lemons are used to flavor stews, while in India, a variety of pickle made with additional spices is served as a condiment. Europeans embraced the piquant Indian version from the moment they tasted it. Writing from India in 1677, a German naturalist by the name of George Eberhard Rumphius described a "delicious pickle" being served with meats and curries. Prepared with spices including coriander, cardamom, cloves, and the pungent *assafoetida,* this treat eventually migrated to Great Britain, where the public heartily embraced it. Lemon pickle remains among the most popular condiments in England today. In Egypt and Syria, the fruit is more likely to be sliced, salted, drained overnight, covered with oil, and eaten as pickles than pickled in brine.

The culinary uses of the lemon eventually caught on in Europe as well, and by the sixteenth century, influential cookbooks began to appear. *Libro Novo,* written by the archbishop of Milan's chef, gave recipes such as Marinated Brill with Lemon Slices, starting the trend of garnishing fish with the colorful fruit that remains popular today. About one hundred years later, *Le cuisinier francais* (1651) was published in France. Written by Pierre François de la Varenne, the squire of the kitchen to the Marquis d'Uxelles, the book marked a turning point in the development of French cooking and was among the first in France to formally make use of the lemon. Heralding classic French cuisine as we know it today, the recipes show a healthy respect for vegetables (unheard of in that day), offer more than sixty ways to prepare eggs, and suggest using lemon juice to sharpen sauces.

In England, the lemon inspired candied sweetmeats and preserves. Early physicians of the Roman empire had written that eating uncooked fruit was dangerous, and the British took this warning to heart. Generally, they believed that fresh fruit brought on sickness, and was particularly to be avoided during epidemics. During one year of pestilence, in 1579, selling fruit on the streets of London was strictly forbidden. As a result, the most popular way to eat fruit in sixteenth-century England was to cook it first with sugar and spices. Fortunately, this was a fine prospect for the lemon, as its tart taste improved with sweetening. By the mid-seventeenth century, lemon jelly had become a popular dessert among the gentry, who adjourned after meals to summer-houses built specifically for the purpose of enjoying such treats. Lemons became an essential ingredient in all sorts of delicacies, such as Taffety Tart, layers of sliced apples strewn with sugar, fennel seed, and finely cut lemon peel, or the more complicated Transparent Pudding, in which layers of sliced almonds, raisins, and candied lemon glisten through a clear jelly mold.

As the birthplace of lemons, India was probably the original site of the first cooling lemon drink, but many delightful variations on the concept have appeared through the ages. The French invented lemonade as we know it around the seventeenth century. The drink of lemon juice mixed with water and sugar, and garnished with lemon slices, quickly caught on throughout Europe. It wasn't long before lemonade sellers in France and Italy began to ply their wares around town—an entrepreneurial idea that children have embraced ever since. Mead, a fermented honey drink flavored with lemon peel and spices, was so well loved by Queen Elizabeth that she carried the beverage with her in jugs when she traveled. Lemon juice was also essential to the British drink called punch, which was made with brandy and sugar. Punch became the preferred drink of the liberal Whigs, while the more conservative Tories stuck with claret.

Along with its versatility in cooking, the lemon has long been known for its medicinal powers. Historical records show that in the nineteenth century, in the Punjab region of India, doctors recommended pickled lemons—cut into thin slices and packed in alternate layers with salt, pounded ginger, and caraway—for treating many medical conditions, including an enlarged spleen. They also mixed pickled lemons with powdered sulfur to make a fine-grained treatment for wounds and skin eruptions. The lemon also had some formidable uses in India—such as giving a blue color to steel swords and making poisons more potent—but on the whole, the fruit contributed only the best kind of healing power.

In the Middle East, the fruit's healing characteristics were first detailed in *The Treatise of the Lemon,* a medical text written by Saladin's physician, Ibn Jamiya. Published in Venice in 1583, the book spread the news of the lemon's therapeutic uses into Italy. Medical men throughout Europe embraced the beneficial properties of the fruit, prescribing decoctions made with lemon juice for ailments ranging from intermittent fever to general weakness. As in India, lemon was used there to treat enlarged spleens. *A Book of Fruits and Flowers,* published in London in 1656, describes many common household uses for lemons, including medical elixirs. One such concoction, a brew made from ale, milk, sorrel, and lemon juice, was proclaimed to be an excellent cure for kidney stones, promising to dissolve the stone and "bring it away." The book also included simple household recipes for lemon syrup and lemon-scented sachets—in the words of the author, "Sweet Bagges to lay amonst Linnen."

Despite their reputation for healing, lemons were not prescribed to prevent scurvy until the end of the eighteenth century. On his round-the-world expedition of 1770 to 1774, George Anson watched as nearly a thousand sailors died of the disease, which caused everything from spongy, bleeding gums to swollen joints and heart failure. For decades, scurvy had killed more British sailors than enemy action had. The first Europeans to make the connection that citrus could cure the disease were probably the Dutch, through their contact with southeast Asian ships that kept citrus on board

during long sea voyages. From the Dutch, the message passed through Europe, and lemon juice became widely recognized as the best cure for scurvy. About twenty years after Anson lost all those sailors to scurvy, the British navy began prescribing mandatory lemon juice rations, and the mortality rate declined sharply.

Sailors often mixed the lemon juice with their rum rations—a neat half pint daily—to make a potent brew. After more than one drunken sailor fell to his death from the rigging, however, the navy decided to reduce the rum ration, and diluted it with lemon juice to make a beverage called grog, which became general issue to sailors in 1795. In the twenty years following grog's invention, the Royal Navy went through more than one and a half million gallons of lemon juice. By the 1850s, juice from limes started replacing that of lemons—leading American seamen to call the British sailors "limeys"— but it proved to be less effective against scurvy, as the juice of limes has considerably less vitamin C than that of lemons or oranges.

the citron

Many experts believe that the lemon is a cross or hybrid of the *citron*. That fruit, which resembles a large lemon with rough skin and has a weak lemon flavor, originated on the Arabian peninsula and was brought to Persia, where the Romans first encountered them in about 500 B.C. The citron revolutionized the way that sourness could be integrated into food, since before its arrival, tart flavors came from less appetizing sources, such as sour apples or the bitter liquid exuded by crushed green wheat. The thick, aromatic peel of the citron is commonly used today for producing an essential oil to scent perfume and, in candied form, for baking.

After the citron reached China around the fourth century A.D., a freak variety developed in which the fruit separated into five lobes that resemble the fingers of a hand. In China, it was considered a symbol of happiness and eventually earned the name "Buddha's hand." The Jews cultivated this unique variety intensively for their religious festivals, and the rare fruit is still used today in the Feast of Tabernacles.

By the nineteenth century, India boasted more types of lemons than perhaps anywhere else in the world, and all of Europe seemed fascinated by this bounty. Captain Lowther, the head of a ship in India, wrote in his ship's journal in 1857, "The various species of oranges and lemons in Assam would astonish you. Lemons of the finest kinds are found wild throughout the forests, and are a great treat to a thirsty, feverish explorer. I often come on a loaded tree in the midst of a grass plain, with no water nearer than some miles. They are doubtless the remains of an ancient civilization." One Italian cookbook from the early nineteenth century suggests, on the subject of making candied lemon peel, that "anybody with leisure, and not in a hurry to make a fortune, might do a good service by experimenting on all the peels of the different varieties of Indian citrus."

Of course, India and the Mediterranean were not alone in providing fertile grounds for lemon cultivation. During the age of European colonization, lemons arrived on distant shores and flourished there. When Columbus arrived in Haiti in 1493 on his second voyage to the New World, the lemon arrived with him, and twenty years later, fruit trees of the highest quality were growing in abundance. During the next fifty years, there was a virtual explosion of lemons in the New World. The Portuguese brought lemons to Brazil, and the Spanish planted the tart golden fruit in San Agostino, their first colony in Florida. Throughout the eighteenth century, the legacy of this cultivation continued. In 1788, the captain of the "First Fleet" of colonists bound for Australia carried lemon trees from Rio de Janeiro to plant once they arrived. Around the same time, Spanish missionaries brought lemon trees to California. It wasn't until the 1849 Gold Rush, however, that lemons started to be cultivated on a wide scale on the west coast of the United States.

Today, the lemon is cultivated worldwide, from India and the Mediterranean to Argentina and Australia, with the United States producing about one-fourth of the world's supply. Used in cuisines around the globe, the lemon is a common sight in both the finest produce market and the cheapest corner store, and is as essential to haute cuisine as it is to home cooking. No longer can it be said, as witty British clergyman Sydney Smith (1771–1845) once famously remarked, "My being in Yorkshire was so far out of the way, that it was actually twelve miles from a lemon."

the essential *lemon*

varieties, uses, and helpful hints

The perfect lemon fits comfortably in one's palm, radiates a bright golden glow and fresh citrus scent, and yields abundant juice and flavorful zest. For much of the year, fruit of this sort can be easily plucked from the bright pyramids at your local produce market, or the branches of your own flourishing tree. Prolific by nature, the *Citrus limon* produces buds, blossoms, and fruit at the same time, revolving continuously through a growth cycle that most plants go through only once a year. Most lemons share the trademark yellow color and oblong shape, but there are numerous varieties, many of which boast delightful, evocative names. The Berna, for example, is the leading lemon in Spain, while the Femminello Ovale is the time-honored Italian favorite. The Nepali Oblong is grown in India, while the Harvey lemon takes its name from Harvey Smith, who discovered the fruit while working in the citrus groves of Clearwater, Florida.

Among so many lemons, which is the fairest of them all? Given ideal growing conditions and warm, sun-drenched landscapes, nearly any variety can produce superior fruit—although the aromatic lemons of the Amalfi Coast are among the most highly prized. Cultivated in cliffside groves above the sparkling Mediterranean, the most common variety, known as Femminello Sfusato, boasts the thick fragrant peel used to flavor the sweet liqueur Limoncello. Fortunately, the Eureka and the Lisbon, the most common North American varieties, can easily achieve perfection as well. At the peak of ripeness, they have well-balanced acid, a bright and slightly rough yellow peel, and about a dozen segments of fine-grained, tender, and juicy pulp. Citrus fans also adore the sweet Meyer lemon, although it's a hybrid of a lemon and a sweet orange, and not a true lemon. Whether your search for the perfect lemon ends at your local farmers' market or the exotic Italian coast, the happy result will be a lovely specimen well suited to many culinary and household uses.

lemons **and** *lemon***like fruits**

Known for their healing properties, lemons are packed with vitamin C, a powerful antioxidant. Hot tea made with lemon juice and honey will soothe a sore throat, and some even drink the juice of a whole lemon each morning. On average, a lemon provides fifty-two milligrams of vitamin C, about half of the daily requirement, as well as trace amounts of beta-carotene and folic acid. The bright yellow, highly acidic type of lemon is the most familiar, but some tree varieties yield unusual forms of the fruit. The Ponderosa, a thick-peeled lemon the size of a grapefruit, is grown for garden ornamentation, while commercial Florida growers cultivate the Avon exclusively for making frozen juice. The most common kitchen and backyard garden lemon varieties are profiled here, along with some familiar lemonlike fruits.

true *lemon*

This is the common, or regular, lemon. The two most widely cultivated true lemons in the United States are the Lisbon and the Eureka. The Lisbon originated in Portugal, reached Australia in 1849, and arrived in California around forty years later. The Eureka, which originated in Italy, arrived in Los Angeles in 1858. The lemon crop from California and Arizona consists mainly of these two varieties and accounts for approximately 25 percent of the world's lemon production. One benefit of the Lisbon is that it has few or no seeds. Neither variety is well adapted to Florida, where the Villafranca, the Bearss, and the Avon are more widely grown. Other leading growers and exporters of true lemons include Italy, Spain, Argentina, Greece, and Turkey, where any number of varieties may be grown, depending on the climate.

rough *lemon* and sweet *lemon*

Although true lemons are the most common type, there are actually two other kinds of lemon: The rough lemon, probably a cross between the lemon and the citron, grows slightly larger than regular size and has a thicker peel. The flesh has a moderate lemon flavor but gives little juice. It is used mostly for rootstock. The sweet lemon, grown in the Mediterranean region and India, more closely resembles the true lemon, but lacks acidity. Neither the rough lemon nor the sweet lemon has much value in the fresh fruit market in North America.

meyer *lemon*

Adored by citrus fans, the sweet hybrid Meyer originated in China and is considered a cross between a true lemon and either an orange or a mandarin. Frank N. Meyer, a plant explorer for the U.S. Department of Agriculture, found the lemon near Peking, where it was cultivated in pots for its ornamental qualities, and brought it back to California in 1908. Today, most Meyer lemons are grown in California's Central Valley, although some fruit also comes from the southern part of the state, Florida, and Texas, where the Meyer has earned the nickname Valley lemon. Meyer lemons appear at produce stands or regional farmers' markets during the peak season, which is generally November, December, and January, and sometimes as late as April, but limited production can make finding them difficult even during these months. The most commonly grown variety is the 'Improved Meyer,' a supposedly disease-free form of the fruit that can be legally grown in California, Texas, and elsewhere. In Arizona, all types of Meyer lemons are illegal and therefore never available, because the trees can harbor a devastating citrus disease known as Citrus Tristeza Virus (CTV), to which it is immune.

Meyers grow to approximately the same size as regular lemons, although larger specimens—with the circumference of a navel orange—sometimes grow in Florida, and can be found in specialty food markets. Meyer lemons make delicious lemonade, slushy Italian lemon granita, and lemon tarts, and their naturally honeyed flavor requires less sweetening than regular, more

acidic lemons. They do retain a slight bite, however, and so provide the perfect substitute for regular lemons on many occasions, whether in preparing a soufflé or for simply squeezing over fresh fish.

mexican lime

Also known as the Key lime, or West Indian lime, this small, oval fruit has a yellow skin at full maturity. Usually harvested before this point, when the fruit is not quite ripe and appears greenish yellow, Mexican limes can resemble a small lemon at first glance—although upon closer inspection, the scent and flavor can be identified as lime. The Mexican lime is easily distinguished from the more widely available Tahitian lime (also called Bearss lime or Persian lime), which has a dark green, glossy skin and is generally larger. Spring is the season for Mexican limes, which are produced on a commercial scale in the Florida Keys, Hawaii, and outside the United States in India, Egypt, Mexico, and the West Indies. Mexican limes can be grown indoors or outdoors where the weather is warm, and they thrive in California.

Mexican limes are used to make the famous Rose's lime juice and are favored by bartenders. They are also the main flavoring in Florida's most famous dessert, Key lime pie, although commercially made versions of the pie often use concentrate made from cheaper, and more widely available, Tahitian limes. The delicious taste of Mexican limes is sure to delight anyone fond of tart citrus, and flavorful rewards await those who seek out the fruit when it is in season.

lemon **harvest**

The ripe golden lemons at your local market may look freshly picked from the tree, but in fact, most lemons are ripened in storage sheds. Using rings to gauge when the fruit reaches a commercially acceptable size, producers harvest lemons while they are still green. The ripening process, known as curing, occurs while the fruit is held in carefully controlled conditions for anywhere from ten days to four months. During this time, the lemon peel becomes thinner and the pulp juicier, and the fruit shrinks slightly and acquires its trademark yellow hue. To speed this color transformation, or degreening, lemons are sometimes exposed to ethylene gas. While the practice is used widely on oranges to intensify color, it's less common with lemons, which tend to suffer deterioration and decay after exposure. Limiting heat and moisture during storage is another essential aspect of curing. In Florida, the high humidity makes storing lemons for more than a couple of weeks difficult, while arid regions like southern California or Arizona provide more ideal conditions.

Commercial lemons supply plenty of juice and have a bright, pleasing appearance, but always look for organic lemons when a recipe calls for peel. Most lemons are exposed to numerous chemical treatments before being shipped: They are often sprayed with pesticides during the growing season, coated with thin layers of fungicide during storage, and lightly varnished with wax. Those people lucky enough to grow lemons at home—where the only shipping and handling happens between the garden and the kitchen—can allow the fruit to ripen on the branch and use it directly after picking, with no need for curing.

lemon oil and lemon wood

Many of the world's lemons are not destined for a fresh fruit market, but are used instead for the highly aromatic and volatile oil in their peel. An essential component of bath and beauty products, lemon oil scents everything from expensive colognes to luxury soaps and shampoos. In West Africa, North Africa, and Italy, lemon tree leaves, twigs, and immature fruits are distilled to make petitgrain oil, which is even more sought after than lemon oil for making perfume. Lemon oil is also an addition to many household cleansers, and for many of us, lemon-scented Pledge brings back memories of shining our family's wooden dining room table. Neither does the wood of the lemon tree go to waste. Fine-grained and pleasant to work with, lemon wood lends itself to small carvings such as chess pieces, toys, or spoons.

how to pick and store *lemons*

To pick the perfect lemon, choose fruit heavy for its size that feels firm to the touch and has bright yellow, unblemished skin. Lemons with thick skin may appear rough or faintly pitted on the surface due to sunken oil glands, while thin-skinned lemons look more uniform and smooth. Rumor has it that lemons with thin skins tend to yield more juice than thicker-skinned varieties, but that is not always the case. As with flavor, the amount of juice depends on the individual fruit itself, where it was cultivated, and when it was picked. Generally, lemons that are heavy for their size will yield the most juice, while thick-skinned varieties are the best choice for preserving, making candied rind, or grating zest. Look for lemons with a well-balanced, elliptical shape, avoiding fruit that appears soft, shriveled, or bruised.

The ideal storage temperature for lemons is about 50°F. Subtropical fruit can be easily damaged by too much cold and suffer chill injuries such as blotching or staining, which can lead to decay. Fortunately, lemons withstand moderate refrigeration quite well, unlike tomatoes, for example, which lose critical flavor components when chilled. Like all fruits and vegetables, lemons are composed mostly of water, and keeping them fresh means preventing moisture loss. The waxy coating sprayed on commercial fruit helps, as does wrapping lemons in plastic or storing them in a refrigerator crisper drawer. Wrapped and chilled, lemons should keep for a month or longer. Bring chilled lemons to room temperature before using.

about juice and zest

Lemons yield the most juice at room temperature, or when slightly warmed. In commercial juice operations, the fruit is immersed in boiling water and blanched briefly before being squeezed, a process that increases the juice yield by as much as 50 percent. For similar results at home, you can immerse the fruit in a bowl of warm water, or even warm it in the microwave on low power for one minute or less. Just before juicing, roll the lemon beneath your hand across a cutting board or counter, using moderate pressure. The typical lemon yields two to three tablespoons of juice. To be safe, purchase more lemons than you need for a particular recipe so you don't run short of juice. Steer clear of bottled varieties. The freshly squeezed juice of regular lemons does the trick every time.

Reaming halved lemons yields more juice than squeezing individual wedges by hand. Use a handheld wooden reamer over a bowl to catch the juice, or a plastic reamer with a saucer. If you don't have either tool, forming a beaklike shape with your fingers and reaming the lemons by hand works nearly as well. In a pinch, a potato ricer can also do the trick—simply cut the lemon into wedges and compress them with the ricer. Lemon juice freezes well, so if you squeeze too much juice, store it in the freezer in an airtight container, or pour into ice trays for cubes.

Highly acidic lemon juice solves all sorts of kitchen dilemmas. A sprinkling prevents sliced fruit from browning and guarantees that trimmed artichokes, which sometimes turn gray during cooking, will keep their lovely green color. The same goes for sliced avocados, which can turn unpleasantly dark after exposure to air. A squeeze of lemon juice provides enough acid to solve the problems caused by alkalinity, such as cake icings turning greenish or, in the case of hard water, hot coffee or tea that looks muddy. Best of all, the powerful acidic properties of lemon juice mean that a few drops go a long way, so the added flavor is slight.

The acid also works as a tenderizer, breaking apart long, stringy protein molecules, making lemon juice an excellent marinade for fish, meat, and poultry. It's also one of the best ways to achieve a light, tender pie crust, since the acids break down the gluten protein in flour. In seviche, a traditional Latin American dish, fresh white fish is "cooked" by the acidic juice of lemons or limes instead of heat. (For an illustration of this potency at home, squeeze a bit of fresh lemon juice over some raw fish and see how quickly the translucent flesh turns opaque.)

A few simple food-science tips will help you use lemon juice with excellent results: It's important to know, for instance, that the acids in lemon juice can prevent sauces from thickening by interfering with how starch molecules

bond. This is the reason to add juice to lemon pie filling *after* it has cooked and thickened, but while the mixture is still hot. (Adding juice once the filling has cooled can cause consistency damage, and adding juice during cooking often results in a thin, watery filling.) In other recipes, such as hollandaise sauce, lemon juice brings important chemistry to the cooking process, diluting the egg yolk mixture just enough to interrupt the usual chemistry so that stovetop heat doesn't scramble the eggs. Fortunately, not all recipes with lemon juice require caution or expertise. Making traditional English lemon curd—the creamy spread used to fill layers of sponge cake, spread on toast or scones, or top lemon bar cookies—takes little precision and is virtually foolproof. Since the tart juice and zest require lots of sweetening, there are plenty of sugar molecules in the custard to prevent the egg proteins from pulling tight and coagulating.

Lemon zest is nearly as versatile as lemon juice. Italian *gremolata*, a blend of zest, garlic, and parsley, tops *osso buco*, hearty bean soup, or delicious fresh fish. Also a good choice for baking, lemon zest delivers intense flavor in small amounts that won't bulk up dough or interfere with the exact ingredient proportions in your recipe. Many lemon desserts require zest as well as juice and use the whole lemon so efficiently that only expressed pulp and bitter pith are left behind. If you are after lemon zest, seek out fruit with thick skin. The waxy coating on commercial fruit can detract from the quality of the peel, so thoroughly wash lemons before zesting for recipes, although an even better option is seeking out organic fruit.

Strips of peel look delicate and translucent after removal from the lemon, but even small amounts contribute robust flavor to recipes. With linguistic flair that brings to mind Dr. Seuss, the French call lemon peel *zeste*, and the white pith beneath *ziste*—more than a rhetorical distinction, since the bitter taste of the pith can ruin the peel's clean, sublime flavor. A swivel-bladed vegetable peeler is among the best tools for obtaining zest without pith, although the resulting strips of peel will require fine chopping for most recipes. You can also grate lemon zest using the smallest holes on a grater, the ones normally used for parmesan cheese. For the most productive and effortless zesting, seek out the microplane-style graters available at cookware stores. As with regular graters, take particular care not to inadvertently grate the pith with the zest. A medium lemon generally yields about two teaspoons of zest.

organic lemons

Cooking with deliciously scented organic lemons can quickly turn regular lemon users into organic converts. Most lemon recipes call for zest, and commercial fruit has a waxy coating that detracts from peel flavor and quality (the same culprit leaves an oily residue on the surface of your hot tea when you add a wedge of lemon). Organic fruit offers pure, uncorrupted peel, and organic orchards tend to be smaller, which generally means higher-quality fruit. Supporting sustainable agriculture is another excellent reason to buy from organic farms, where lemon groves stay healthy with natural solutions instead of synthetic pesticides. Organic growers often work with cooperative insectaries, pest-management organizations that supply beneficial parasitic wasps or lacewings to help keep orchards healthy, or introduce anemic earthworms to the soil. The earthworms feed on decomposing plant material, their droppings enhance the soil's nutrient status, and their burrowing techniques improve soil structure, which can lead to overall water savings for the grove.

Lemons are a popular crop among organic farmers in California, perhaps because organic orchards yield numbers similar to conventionally produced crops: between five hundred and nine hundred 55-pound field boxes per acre. Organic farming represents only a tiny fraction of the state's overall agriculture, but continued demand is helping it to grow steadily. Shopping for organic fruit not only is sound for the earth, but it will also make your culinary ventures with lemon zest a resounding success.

from tree to table

easy backyard and container gardening

The joy of gardening with lemons begins the moment you plunge your hands in the cool garden soil, and continues throughout the seasons. Replete with glossy green leaves, aromatic white blossoms, and juicy golden fruit, the flourishing lemon tree provides many delights for gardeners in warm climates. Equally suited to formal gardens, small backyards, and container pots, the lemon is among the easiest citrus to grow. Given a spot with plenty of sun, the tree only requires simple basics such as watering, fertilizing, and frost protection to thrive. From the novelty Ponderosa to the classic Eureka lemon, there are many delightful types to choose from, and all varieties boast lovely foliage that ornaments the garden even when the tree does not bear fruit. Whether your interest is backyard growing or indoor cultivation, this chapter provides inspiration for the potential lemon gardener, along with plenty of practical advice for keeping your tree productive and healthy.

Among the most timeless elements of garden design, the lemon tree provides a link between ancient landscapes and contemporary gardens. Integrated into courtyards and orchards from ancient Rome to Moorish Spain to Renaissance Europe, the flowering tree has long been considered a symbol of love and courtship. In the seventeenth century, Persian miniature paintings illustrating ancient Arabic poetry showed princesses and their suitors lounging beneath boughs laden with bright golden fruit. But while writers and painters dreamed of romance, gardeners and botanists concerned themselves with the practical aspects of cultivation, with remarkable results. Many of the most effective techniques for growing lemons are quite literally ancient history. Patterns of cultivation from centuries ago have striking similarities to the approaches taken today, starting with the classical layout of lemons in the sunny peristyle courtyards of Pompeii. In the fifteenth century, Italians planted lemons on warm, south-facing slopes, or in containers that could be moved to protective sheds *(stanzone limonaie)* for the winter. Situating lemon trees against a warm garden wall was another common technique that is still practiced today.

In the sixteenth century, grafting trees onto dwarf rootstock became quite common. Published in Florence in 1552, *La grande arte della agricultura* by Girolamo Fiorenzuola explicitly discusses the benefits of dwarf fruit trees and encourages using them for garden ornamentation. Small in stature but highly productive, the popular trees were planted everywhere from the famous Boboli Gardens in Italy to the Leiden Botanical Garden in Holland. As the tree gained recognition, so did its numerous varieties, and Agostino del Riccio's *Del Giardino di un Re,* published in 1597, suggests fourteen different types of lemon suitable for decorating courtyards. More botanical details appear in Giovanni Battista Ferratis's *Hesperides,* published in 1646, the first book devoted entirely to citrus and the many types of orange, lemon, citron, and lime.

In cold climates north of the Alps, only the wealthiest gardeners could cultivate citrus, which required heated houses—and at first, the trees generally refused to fruit, although improved heating techniques eventually solved this problem. By the late seventeenth century, the one hundred–acre Brompton Park Nursery in London had a thriving collection of various lemons. In Victorian England, greenhouses called orangeries sheltered lemons and other exotic fruits. Viewed as status symbols, the structures required great wealth to construct and maintain.

In the New World, the Spanish first planted the lemon tree in the warm, embracing soil of Mexico. It was then introduced to California by the Franciscans, when they established the first Spanish mission in San Diego in 1769. The lemon tree appeared consistently in the gardens of the twenty-one Spanish missions built along the coast, adorning high-walled, exquisitely planned grounds that also boasted luxurious blooming roses and fruiting figs and olives. When California became a state in 1846, the lemon spread outside the garden walls and into commercial production.

By the middle of the nineteenth century, large plantings were also common in Florida—until the devastating freezes of 1886 and 1894 delivered fatal blows to the industry. Mostly because of weather, but also because the humid climate made curing difficult and the lemons were prone to scab, large-scale cultivation in Florida collapsed. Not until the 1950s, when the need for processed lemon products like juice and cold-press lemon oil increased, did commercial lemon cultivation in the state revive. On a smaller scale, however, the lemon remained a permanent fixture in Florida and throughout the South. Nineteenth-century plans for an ornamental garden in Charleston, South Carolina, designed by the sons of famous Central Park landscape architect Frederick Law Olmsted, included a hearty fruiting lemon (*Citrus trifoliata*); today this tree is still widely grown in that region.

Meanwhile, in the chillier northeastern states, it wasn't until the late 1800s that the ordinary gardener had access to all the plants in Europe, and started growing the tender varieties that required the protection of greenhouses. In the twentieth century, American gardening trends shifted away from expensive, exotic species toward native plants. Now, however, botanical gardens around the United States are showing renewed interest in housing citrus and tropical fruits in old world–style orangeries, contributing to the cycle that connects the lemon gardeners of yesterday with those of today.

backyard *lemon* tending

Warm or hot summers paired with mild winters provide the best growing conditions for lemons, but a home grower can also succeed in cooler climates where commercial production would be impossible. Lemons flourish in the low deserts of southern California and Arizona, and California's Central Valley. Protected from winter cold spells, lemons can easily grow in the cooler,

Northern California summers, and prosper as far north as Mendocino. In cool areas along the coast, the hearty Meyer lemon does particularly well. Whether you're choosing a lemon tree for your yard or need tips for keeping the foliage healthy, this section offers the techniques necessary to start down the garden path. (For information on container gardening with lemons, see pages 40–41)

Nearly all lemon trees are composites, consisting of two genetically different varieties of citrus grafted together. A rootstock, or understock, forms the base of the tree. The best rootstocks tolerate pests and disease well and adapt to adverse soil conditions, while tops, known as scions, are selected for fruit quality. Grafted trees produce fruit within a few years, unlike seedling trees, which can take ten or fifteen years. Standard lemon trees are grown on a variety of rootstocks and grow to twenty or thirty feet. Dwarf lemon trees, typically grown on rootstock called trifoliate orange *(Poncirus trifoliata)*, usually grow to between eight and fifteen feet. "Flying Dragon," a variety of trifoliate orange, produces even smaller trees and is the most common rootstock for container lemons. Look closely at the lemon trees at your local nursery—the graft point, or bud union, where the top was grafted onto the rootstock, will be clearly visible.

garden varieties

The Eureka and the Lisbon are the most common lemons in western gardens. Both trees grow to about twenty feet, with attractively dense foliage and large, dark green leaves, and bear fruit all year in warm climates. Nearly all lemon trees have some spiky thorns, although the Eureka has fewer than the Lisbon. Given ideal growing conditions, either of these trees will produce more lemons then one home can handle, providing a surplus to delight friends and neighbors. Eureka and Lisbon lemons are nearly identical in size, flavor, and taste. The Lisbon is more resistant to cold and adapts better to high heat, making it the best choice for Arizona.

For those interested in moving beyond the regular lemon, there are many elegant trees that lend themselves to landscaping. The 'Sungold' variety, a semidwarf tree that grows to about fourteen feet tall and eight feet wide, has

green leaves dappled with cream color, and yellow fruit adorned with green stripes. The 'Variegated Pink' is the formal name of the lemon variety also known as 'Pink Lemonade.' It has green-and-white mottled leaves, and a green-and-white striped immature fruit that ripens to yellow, with a rosy pink interior.

The Ponderosa lemon is a very mild-flavored, rough-skinned large fruit that can grow larger than a grapefruit and weigh up to several pounds. An attractive novelty, the Ponderosa makes an intriguing addition to the garden, although the fruit can't substitute for true lemons in practical use. Productive at a young age, most heavily in winter, it has open, angular branches with widely spaced leaves. The dwarf tree reaches about four to six feet, while the regular version will grow to about twice that size.

A darling among citrus lovers, the Meyer lemon is an excellent tree for regions with mild winters and slightly cooler summers, such as Northern California, and is considerably more cold resistant than the true lemon. 'Improved Meyer' is the variety grown in California, Texas, Hawaii, and else-where, although in Arizona, Meyer lemons cannot be legally grown because of citrus disease precautions. Meyer trees yield juicy fruit year-round, and begin to bear lemons at a very young age. At regular size, the tree generally grows to about twelve feet tall and fifteen feet wide, while dwarf trees will generally hit only eight feet.

sunlight

Grow lemons in full sun. They can survive in semishade, but full sun will produce stronger growth and more fruit. The trees should also be protected from wind.

soil drainage

Well-drained soil is the key to keeping lemon trees healthy. If planting out-doors, test soil-drainage capacity by digging a two-foot-deep hole and filling it with water. Refill it whenever it drains throughout the day, and the following day refill it again—if several hours pass and the water does not recede, plant the lemon tree elsewhere, or on a raised mound or bed. Improve average soil, or prevent sandy soil from retaining too much water, by digging in a five-inch layer of garden compost or ground bark to a depth of about one foot.

watering practices

Water newly planted trees twice a week in normal summer weather, more often when it gets extremely hot. Established trees should be watered every other week during summer. Be consistent with your watering, and don't let the tree reach the wilting point. The soil should never feel bone dry, and there should never be standing water. The biggest danger in overwatering happens in clay soil, where air space is tight.

freeze protection

There are many ways to shelter outdoor trees during a cold snap. Among the most convenient is draping the tree with strings of Christmas lights and lightweight, woven polyester row cover. This approach takes little time and effort, because you can drape items directly over the tree with good results, unlike heavier canvas or plastic, which can cause freezing if it comes in contact with the leaves. However, without any lightweight row cover on hand, the job is easily accomplished by draping protective plastic or burlap over poles or stakes surrounding the tree. Doublecheck that the covering does not touch the leaves. You may want to add a heat source like a Coleman lantern, although for safety, make sure the lamp doesn't touch the tree or the covering. Spraying leaves with antitranspirant spray will give the tree a few degrees of frost protection, but the best plan is to physically shelter it from the cold.

planting

While the general advice is not to disturb citrus roots before planting, examine the root ball closely before placing a lemon tree in the ground. Loosen any excessive matting beneath the ball, or any encircling main roots that could potentially choke off root growth. Container trees purchased from a nursery are sometimes grown in a soilless medium and benefit from being washed off with a gentle stream of water. This also exposes peripheral roots, which helps them make immediate contact with the surrounding soil once they are planted. You may also want to work garden soil through the root ball

before placing in the ground to further encourage growth in new soil. Always water thoroughly after planting.

When planting, be sure the bud union, the point at which the scion unites with the rootstock, is well above the level of the soil. As a general guideline, plant the tree at about the same depth that it was planted in its nursery container. Several inches of mulch over the soil is a good idea, particularly since some roots grow near the surface. Always keep the area beneath the tree canopy free of grass and other plants.

using fertilizers

Once the tree begins showing strong growth, fertilize periodically with nitrogen, always watering well beforehand. Nitrogen is essential for lemon trees to flourish. In areas where freezes are common, the first feeding should be in late winter, and fertilization should stop at the end of summer when the weather starts turning colder. Prevent iron, manganese, or zinc deficiencies, which can cause leaves to yellow, by spraying the tree with a foliar spray containing all three nutrients.

pruning

Branches that sprout below the graft line, or bud union, are called suckers and should be removed right away. They belong to the rootstock variety and never bear fruit. Prune frost-damaged trees late in the spring or summer, when you can easily tell new growth from deadwood. Prune full-size Lisbon and Eureka trees to keep the fruit easily reachable. Wear long sleeves and protective gloves when pruning, since lemon trees have thorns.

In desert regions or other areas with extreme sun exposure, protect limbs or trunks newly exposed after pruning. Paint with a protective layer of whitewash or latex paint diluted with 50 percent water.

harvesting fruit

Ripe fruit should come off the tree with a gentle tug, and be picked only when it reaches an acceptable size. Lemon trees are most heavily productive in winter and spring, although in good climate conditions the trees fruit throughout the year. On newly planted trees, pick fruit right away to channel energy into new growth rather than fruiting.

easy container gardening

With their glossy green leaves and delightful scent, potted lemon trees can thrive in a sunny household nook or outdoors on the patio. Look for dwarf trees on 'Flying Dragon' rootstock, which usually grow to six or seven feet. The general guidelines for growing lemons in containers are similar to those used for outdoor trees (see pages 33–39), but this section includes important tips and techniques specifically for keeping container plants healthy.

In the mildest climates of Southern California and Arizona, potted lemon trees can stay outdoors all winter. In freeze-prone areas, pay careful attention to weather warnings and move containers indoors when the forecast calls for low temperatures. In winter, store them in a cool greenhouse or any sheltered area, such as a basement or garage, that gets plenty of sun.

One of the most popular citrus plants to grow in pots is the 'Improved Meyer' lemon. This variety is a disease-free form, and legal in California, Texas, Hawaii, and elsewhere. (Both the original and improved varieties are illegal in Arizona, since they can harbor a powerful citrus disease.) The dwarf trees can grow up to eight feet tall, so be sure you have enough room. Another variety suited to containers is the dwarf Ponderosa, which should reliably produce healthy fruit even when planted in a container.

Plant lemon trees in containers with a diameter of at least one and a half feet. Choose a container you can move without too much difficulty, because the lemon tree should be moved outside during the summer and protected indoors when the weather turns chilly.

Well-drained soil is among the most important basics of keeping the plant healthy. Double-check that the container and potting soil provide adequate drainage. Potting soil for African violets or roses can suit them quite well, but the best idea is to ask for soil recommendations at your local nursery.

Indoors, keep lemon trees close to a sunny window, preferably not farther than six feet away. Avoid placing them near radiators or other direct heat sources.

Daily misting, surrounding the tree with pebble trays filled with water, or using a humidifier can prevent it from dropping flowers and fruits, a problem that is often caused by low humidity. Lemon trees do best with humidity at about 50 percent.

In normal weather, water twice a week. In very hot summer weather, you may need to water potted lemons daily, particularly when they are outdoors. Do not overwater in winter; allow the soil to dry slightly between waterings. Never allow standing water.

When bringing lemon trees outside for the first time in spring, place them in the shade first, then slowly increase their exposure to direct sunlight.

When plants are kept indoors, you will need to pollinate the flowers by hand. Using a small paintbrush, gently transfer the pollen from the stamens to the pistil in the center of the bloom of each flower. Deadheading isn't necessary, since eventually the blooms will fade and drop off, and be replaced by fruit.

Lemon trees in containers generally do not require much pruning, although you should remove dead or damaged branches, and of course, suckers growing from the rootstock.

At a minimum, root-prune and repot potted lemon trees in fresh soil every four or five years. There is no need to enlarge the pot unless you wish to encourage growth, in which case you can repot the tree annually into a slightly bigger pot until it reaches the desired size. Repot trees in spring, and keep them away from too much direct sunlight in the weeks immediately afterward.

countering common problems

The tree will not bloom.

If you have been repotting the tree every year into a slightly larger container, allow the tree to remain in the same-size pot for two or three years and don't repot until the plant has bloomed. The lovely flowers and fruit are worth the wait, and attempting to transfer the nonblooming tree back to a smaller pot will not solve the problem. Another reason behind the lack of blooms could be a lack of sunlight.

Leaves are yellowing and dropping off.

Overwatering often causes this problem. Water molds cause root rot, which shows up in yellowing and dropping foliage. Correcting your watering schedule should solve the problem. Mottled or yellowish leaves can also signal deficiencies in iron, zinc, or manganese. Fertilize with products that contain all three nutrients. Yellowish leaves can also be due to nitrogen deficiency, although you should be wary of overdoing the nitrogen fertilizer, which will give the dark leaves the appearance of burned tips or edges.

The fruit looks abnormal and poorly formed.

One likely culprit is the citrus mite, which can be controlled with horticultural oil spray used in the spring or fall. Avoid spraying trees during hot summer weather.

The lower trunk bark is splayed out, and some wood appears rotten.

When a lemon tree is planted too low in the soil, moisture collects around the bud union, causing a fungus known as *collar rot*. To counter the problem, use a sharp tool to remove the rotted wood, spray with a copper spray, and cover the area with pruning paint.

lemon-**scented herbs**

Lemon-scented grasses and herbs contribute a delightful, refreshing citrus aroma to food and drink, and keep for months in the pantry. The Lemon Herb Windowsill Garden (page 109) is a quick craft project with lemon-scented plants that are easy to care for. This overview describes various uses and general instructions for growing.

lemon balm, *melissa officinalis*

The citrus-scented leaves of this green herb have potent medicinal properties. When dried, the leaves brew delicious tea that is recommended as a digestive aid. You can find the dried version in stores or grow the plant yourself. Lemon balm will thrive indoors, planted in a container or pot, and grows new leaves continuously throughout the year, so long as the temperature doesn't dip below 45°F. Outdoors, this perennial grows best in full sun or partial shade, with regular water. Lemon balm can spread rapidly and overwhelm other plants, so clip occasionally to keep the plant compact. It usually grows to about two feet tall and one and a half feet wide. Species that offer variations on the normally light green foliage include types with solid yellow leaves, or green leaves variegated in yellow. The white and yellow flowers that appear on the plant in summer tend to attract bees.

*lemon*grass, *cymbopogon citratus*

Also known as citronella, lemongrass has fibrous, straw-colored stalks that impart a slightly sour flavor to many Southeast Asian dishes. The tough and bitter grass is not eaten whole, but is used for its unique, strong flavor, particularly in Thai curry paste and soups. When preparing lemongrass, trim away the gray-green blades of grass, and slice or grind the stem to use as a flavoring. Available in specialty and Asian markets, lemongrass stalks should appear unblemished and firm, and will keep in the refrigerator wrapped in plastic for up to two months. Lemongrass can be grown in regions with very mild winters, such as the low desert areas of California and Arizona; it prefers full sun and regular water. In most regions, the plant will do best

when protected indoors over winter. Lemongrass has a bulbous root base, and grows in clumps of inch-wide leaves that reach three to four feet tall.

lemon thyme, *thymus* x *citriodorus*

Combining the heady scent of regular thyme with the zesty aroma of lemon, this herb has countless uses in the kitchen, from seasoning chicken or fish to preparing hot tea to ease colds and congestion. A prolific grower, lemon thyme is a perfect choice for a simple herb garden or window box. Fresh lemon thyme will keep for a week, wrapped in damp towels in the refrigerator. The whole dried leaves will keep up to a year, and the ground version should be replaced every six months for maximum flavor. A member of the mint family, lemon thyme thrives easily provided with well-drained soil and sun (it may require partial shade in very hot climates). Generally, it grows to about one foot high and two feet wide. The plant has lovely lavender flowers in summer, and some varieties boast green leaves splashed with streaks of silver or gold.

lemon verbena, *aloysia triphylla*

Offering perhaps the most intense flavor of the many lemon-scented plants, lemon verbena leaves have an unmistakably sharp, puckery scent. Lemon verbena tea, which can be made with dried or fresh leaves, makes a refreshing citrusy beverage. To store fresh leaves, wrap them in plastic and refrigerate, and use within two or three days. If using dried leaves, widely available in stores, replace every few months to ensure maximum potency. The plant prefers warmth, but in western gardens will grow as far north as Seattle, given a sheltered corner or warm garden wall. In colder climates, it succeeds best as a houseplant, particularly when pinched frequently and carried outdoors in summer months. Native to Chile and Argentina, this leggy shrub can reach six feet tall and six feet wide. Putting low plants around the base can disguise its gangly look, or it can be trained and clipped into a hedge. Lemon verbena bears narrow three-inch leaves along the branches, and pretty white flowers in summer.

cooking with *lemons*

Few ingredients match the versatility of lemons. In addition to their own clean, sunny flavor, lemons intensify the flavors of other ingredients—and nothing dresses up a dish more simply and elegantly than a lemon slice or spiraling strip of zest. This chapter features recipes for drinks, sauces, savory snacks, and sweet treats that showcase lemons not only for their characteristic flavor, but for their undeniable visual appeal as well.

lemon **vodka**

Here's one of the easiest and most beautiful gifts you'll ever make. It's also one of the most delicious, so be sure to make a batch for yourself as well. Lemon vodka is delicious sipped on its own, or mixed into a Lemon Drop Cocktail (facing page). Store it in the freezer and serve it ice cold.

Remove the labels from a fifth (750 ml) of vodka, or decant the vodka into a clean, decorative bottle. Use a lemon zester to remove the zest from a lemon in one long, spiraling strand. Drop the lemon peel into the bottle, seal, and let sit at room temperature for about a week before using.

Yield: One 750 ml bottle

lemon vodka in a decorative ice block

For an impressive presentation, freeze a bottle of lemon vodka in a lemon-and-herb-studded block of ice. Cut the top off of a clean, half-gallon milk carton and set the bottle in the center. Fill the carton about halfway with water. Push lemon slices, sprigs of fresh herbs, strands of lemon zest, and lemon blossoms into the water around all four sides. Freeze until solid. When the bottom layer is completely frozen, add enough water to come up to the middle of the neck of the bottle and pack in more lemon slices and herbs. Freeze overnight. To serve, peel away the milk carton and discard. Set the vodka ice block on a small waterproof tray to protect your table and have a cloth napkin or towel handy for lifting the bottle to pour.

For a cold-weather presentation, use lemon slices, sprigs of evergreen, and fresh cranberries to decorate the ice block.

lemon **drop cocktail**

If ever there was a reason for keeping a supply of lemon sugar and lemon vodka on hand, this is it. This cocktail can be thrown together in minutes, yet the simple and elegant presentation will make it look like you hired a bartender for the evening.

¼ cup lemon sugar (recipe follows) or regular sugar
1 lemon wedge, plus slices for garnishing
1½ ounces citron vodka or lemon vodka (facing page)
¾ ounce freshly squeezed lemon juice

Spread all but 1 teaspoon of the lemon sugar out on a saucer. Run the lemon wedge around the rim of a cocktail glass. Invert the glass and dip into the lemon sugar, coating the entire rim. (You will have sugar left over, enough to coat the rims of 2 or 3 more glasses.)

Combine the vodka, lemon juice, and remaining 1 teaspoon of lemon sugar and shake with cracked ice. Strain into the sugar-rimmed glass and garnish with a lemon slice.

Yield: 1 drink

lemon sugar

Combine the grated zest of 4 large lemons (avoid the bitter white pith) with 3 cups of sugar. Store in a tightly covered jar for up to 1 month.

Yield: about 3 cups

Note: Lemon sugar makes a quickly assembled and welcome gift for anyone who enjoys cooking. It performs culinary magic when added to baked goods, fruit desserts, hot or cold tea, and cocktails. Fill a cork-stoppered glass canister or antique canning jar with the sugar and tie it up with a wide yellow ribbon. Attach a hardmade card listing some of its uses, if you like.

sparkling *lemonade*
with *lemon*-slice daisies

Seltzer water adds effervescence to this classic beverage. Easy-to-make lemon-slice daisies add a festive note, and are equally lovely floating in the pitcher or garnishing individual glasses.

One **6**-ounce can frozen lemonade concentrate, thawed

2 large lemons

1 quart seltzer water, chilled

Pour the lemonade concentrate into a pitcher. Squeeze in the juice of one lemon. Just before serving, pour the chilled seltzer into the pitcher and stir to mix. Taste and adjust the flavor, adding:

- more lemon juice or a little sugar, depending on your preference
- a splash of grenadine for pink lemonade
- a splash of Lemon Vodka (page 48) to make an adult beverage
- a handful of blueberries to make polka-dot lemonade

Use the remaining lemon to make the daisy garnishes. To make a daisy, cut a lemon slice ¼ inch thick. Scallop the edges by using a sharp knife to cut out little triangles all around the edge of the rind.

Yield: 4 to 6 servings

honey *lemon* chips

A fun alternative to the more traditional candied lemon peel, these sweet-and-sour lemon slices are delicious on their own, or as a pretty garnish for citrus-flavored desserts. To make a unique gift for a lemon lover, decorate a plain cellophane bag or small galvanized tin with vintage lemon stickers, fill with lemon chips, and tie with a pretty ribbon.

3 lemons
2½ cups sugar
3 tablespoons honey

Use a very sharp knife (a serrated bread knife works well) to cut the lemons into paper-thin slices. You need to end up with slices that are the same thickness and about the same diameter, so cut the ends of the lemons off and save them for another use. Remove all seeds and discard. Place 2 cups of the sugar and 1 cup of water in a large, heavy skillet. Add the honey and bring to a boil over medium heat. Watch the syrup and shake the skillet gently, but do not stir. Boil for 3 minutes or until the sugar is completely dissolved and the syrup is clear. Lower the heat to a simmer and add the lemon slices in a single layer.

Cook the slices for about 45 minutes, maintaining the lowest possible simmer. (Boiling the slices may cause them to fall apart.) Turn the skillet from time to time or use a wooden skewer to slide the slices around so they all cook evenly. The cooked slices will be quite pliable. Carefully remove them from the liquid with a slotted spatula and place on a parchment-lined baking sheet to cool.

Line another baking sheet with parchment and cover it with the remaining ½ cup sugar. When the slices are cool and slightly hardened, dip them in the bed of sugar, lightly coating both sides.

The lemon chips can be kept in an airtight container in the refrigerator for several months, or can be stored in the freezer indefinitely.

Yield: 20 to 25 chips

Note: The sugar syrup left over from making the lemon slices can be boiled down to make a version of Citrus Suckers (page 68).

lemon-**parsley biscuits**

Lemon zest really brings out the flavor of parsley, making these biscuits perfect for serving with roast chicken or simply prepared fish. Hand-cutting the dough gives the biscuits an old-fashioned, rustic appeal. If you prefer to use a biscuit cutter, discard the scraps, as rerolled biscuit dough tends to make tougher biscuits. Or, bake the irregularly shaped scraps in a separate pan for a quick snack.

2 cups flour
1 teaspoon baking powder
½ teaspoon baking soda
½ teaspoon salt
½ cup (**1** stick) cold unsalted butter, cut into small pieces
3 tablespoons chopped fresh parsley
2 teaspoons grated or finely chopped lemon zest
⅔ cup milk

Preheat the oven to 425°F. In a medium bowl, combine the flour, baking powder, baking soda, and salt and stir to mix. Using a pastry blender or your fingers, cut in the butter until the mixture resembles coarse meal. Stir in the parsley and lemon zest. Add the milk and stir until the dough comes together in a cohesive mass. Transfer the dough to a lightly floured surface and knead gently 6 to 8 times.

Pat or roll the dough into an 8-inch square about ½ inch thick. Using a sharp knife, cut the dough into 2-inch squares and place them on a parchment-lined baking sheet. Bake for 15 to 20 minutes, or until lightly browned.

Yield: 16 biscuits

Note: For a quicker, healthier version, omit the butter (and the pastry blender process) and substitute ½ cup of olive oil. Just pour in the oil when you add the milk. This fragrant olive oil version is especially good with Italian or Mediterranean-inspired dishes.

classic hollandaise sauce

Making hollandaise is simply a matter of using extremely low, gentle heat to warm egg yolks until they thicken slightly, and then slowly whisking in melted butter to make a rich, creamy sauce. If the yolks get too hot, they will scramble. Some cooks prefer to use a water bath or double boiler, but a heavy saucepan is sufficient as long as you pay close attention. While it can be a bit tricky, the payoff is well worth the effort. Aside from its classic role in Eggs Benedict, this buttery-rich yet lemony-light emulsion is a brilliant accompaniment to asparagus, artichokes, broccoli, and baked fish.

¾ cup (1½ sticks) unsalted butter
3 large egg yolks
3 tablespoons water
1½ tablespoons strained fresh lemon juice
½ teaspoon salt
Pinch of white pepper

In a small saucepan, melt the butter and set aside. In a heavy, nonreactive saucepan, beat the egg yolks, water, lemon juice, and salt and pepper with a whisk until the yolks are slightly paler in color, about 2 minutes. Place the saucepan over the lowest possible heat. (At no point should the base of the pan be too hot to touch.) Stir the yolks constantly with the whisk as they slowly begin to thicken. When the mixture begins to hold the trail of the whisk for about 3 seconds, it is sufficiently thickened. Remove the pan from the heat.

While beating constantly, add the warm butter by drops until the sauce begins to thicken. After you have added about a tablespoon of the butter by drops, you may begin to add it by teaspoons, still beating constantly. (If the butter is added too quickly, the sauce may break or the emulsion may be too thin.)

Once all the butter has been added, adjust the seasonings. If the sauce is too thick, thin it with a few drops of water or lemon juice. Serve immediately or hold up to 30 minutes in a warm spot on the stove or in a pan of tepid water. The sauce should be warm, not hot.

Yield: about 1¼ cups

flavored butters

Even butter benefits from a little lemon. The possibilities for compound butters are virtually endless. Savory butters are delicious melted atop potatoes, meat, or fish, or simply tossed with pasta. Sweet butters are a divine addition to humble toast. Use the following suggestions as a springboard for your own creations. Compound butters freeze well for up to 3 months.

lemon-herb butter

In a small bowl, beat ¹/₂ cup (1 stick) softened unsalted butter with 1 teaspoon lemon juice and 1¹/₂ teaspoons *each* grated or finely chopped lemon zest, minced fresh parsley, and minced fresh chives. Form into a log, wrap in plastic wrap, and store in the refrigerator. Serve on steamed vegetables such as asparagus, broccoli, corn on the cob, or peas, or as a topper for any simply prepared fish. Use within 4 days or freeze.

Yield: ¹/₂ cup

lemon-wine butter

In a small saucepan, cook 1 tablespoon minced shallots in ¹/₂ cup red wine over medium-high heat until reduced by half. Remove from heat and add ¹/₂ teaspoon grated or finely chopped lemon zest, 1 tablespoon minced fresh parsley, and a generous pinch *each* of dried tarragon and freshly ground black pepper. Let cool. In a small bowl, combine the wine mixture with ¹/₂ cup (1 stick) softened unsalted butter. Pack into a small crock and refrigerate. Use on broiled steaks, chops, or roast beef. Use within 1 week or freeze.

Yield: ³/₄ cup

lemon marmalade butter

In a small bowl, combine ¹/₂ cup Meyer Lemon Marmalade (page 83) with ¹/₂ cup (1 stick) softened unsalted butter. Form into a log, wrap in plastic wrap, and store in the refrigerator. Use as a spread for toast, bagels, biscuits, muffins, or pancakes. Use within 2 weeks or freeze. If you haven't prepared the Meyer Lemon Marmalade, substitute your favorite store-bought preserve or marmalade.

Yield: 1 cup

preserved *lemons*

Unusually tart and salty, preserved lemons are a perfect accompaniment to cold roasted meats or grilled fish. Use them to flavor soups and stews, or make a fresh-flavored hors d'oeuvre by topping pita points with slivers of the lemons, chopped red onions, mint leaves, and a drizzle of olive oil.

3 large, firm lemons
¼ cup sea salt
1 cinnamon stick
1½ teaspoons coriander seeds
½ teaspoon black peppercorns
12 whole cloves

Bring a large saucepan of water to a boil and add the whole lemons. Return to a boil and cook for 3 minutes. Remove the lemons with a slotted spoon and plunge them into cold water.

Empty and rinse out the saucepan, then combine 2½ cups water with the salt, cinnamon stick, coriander seeds, and peppercorns in the pan and bring the mixture to a rolling boil. Turn off the heat and set aside.

Pat the cooled lemons dry. Cut each lemon into quarters, vertically, leaving the quarters attached at the stem end. Pierce the center of the rind of each quarter with a wooden skewer or the tip of a small knife and stud with a clove. Put the lemons in a warm, sterilized, wide-mouthed quart jar. Reheat the spice mixture to just boiling and pour it over the lemons, filling the jar. Tuck the cinnamon stick into the jar and seal.

Let stand for 6 weeks before using. Once the jar is opened the lemons will keep, refrigerated, for several months.

Yield: 1 quart

Note: Because of their natural beauty, preserved lemons need very little packaging to make an impression. Present them in vintage canning jars or check your cookware store for unique glass containers such as German glass-lidded, spring-clamp canning jars. Attach a snip of pretty ribbon to the top with a bit of sealing wax.

vinaigrette trio

Good-quality, extra-virgin olive oil and freshly squeezed lemon juice are key ingredients to a good vinaigrette. For an added dimension, substitute this flavored oil for regular olive oil: Thread alternating lemon wedges (seeds discarded) and peeled garlic cloves onto a wooden skewer. Stand the skewer in a tall glass jar, add a small handful of black peppercorns, fill to the top with olive oil, and cap. Let sit for 1 week before using. This lemon-pepper oil is as pretty to look at as it is delicious, and makes a lovely gift.

classic *lemon*-balsamic vinaigrette

3 tablespoons freshly squeezed lemon juice
1 tablespoon balsamic vinegar
1 tablespoon whole-grain mustard
Pinch of sugar
¾ cup olive oil
2 tablespoons finely chopped parsley
1 large clove garlic, peeled and smashed
Salt and freshly ground black pepper, to taste

In a small bowl, combine the lemon juice, vinegar, mustard, and sugar. Gradually whisk in the olive oil in a thin stream. Add the parsley, garlic clove, and salt and pepper. Remove the garlic clove before serving.

Yield: about 1 cup

lemon-soy vinaigrette

3 roasted garlic cloves
2 tablespoons freshly squeezed lemon juice
1 tablespoon red wine vinegar
2 teaspoons soy sauce
Freshly ground black pepper, to taste
⅓ cup olive oil
2 teaspoons sesame oil

In a small bowl. use a fork to mash the roasted garlic. Add the lemon juice, vinegar, soy sauce, and pepper. Gradually whisk in the oils in a thin stream.

Yield: about ¾ cup

warm *lemon*-maple vinaigrette

2 tablespoons olive oil
1 shallot, chopped
¼ cup *each* freshly squeezed lemon juice, apple-cider vinegar, and pure maple syrup
Salt and freshly ground black pepper, to taste

In a skillet, heat the oil over medium-high heat. Add the shallot and cook, stirring, until softened, about 4 minutes. Add the lemon juice, vinegar, and syrup and bring to a boil. Season with salt and pepper. Pour the hot dressing over hearty greens like spinach to make a warm, wilted salad.

Yield: about 1 cup

oil-cured olives

The natural beauty of olives and herbs inspires elegant preparations that make wonderful gifts. After a few days, the oil in which the olives marinate becomes highly flavored and can be used on its own to drizzle over salads or for cooking.

Using a sharp knife, or a swivel-blade vegetable peeler, remove the zest of 1 lemon (without removing the white pith). Set lemon aside for another use. Place 2 cups Niçoise or Kalamata olives (drained of any liquid) and the zest in a sterilized, wide-mouthed quart jar. Wash and dry 4 to 6 sprigs of fresh herbs such as tarragon, rosemary, thyme, bay leaf, and/or parsley and push them into the jar. Fill the jar to the top with a good-quality olive oil (about 1 cup) and cap. Refrigerate and use within 1 month. Shake the jar occasionally to redistribute the contents.

Yield: 1 quart

Note: Depending on availability and personal taste, almost any fresh herb can be used in this recipe. Basil is risky, however, as it can turn black in the oil. Pick herbs early in the morning and choose young growth that hasn't flowered yet.

gremolata

This simple, fresh seasoning blend is a traditional finish for classic Italian dishes like *osso buco*. Try it on stews and simple pastas or stirred into mashed potatoes.

Combine ¹/₂ cup chopped fresh flat-leaf (Italian) parsley with 2 tablespoons freshly grated lemon zest and 4 minced garlic cloves. Season with salt and pepper. Serve within 1 hour.

Yield: about ¹/₂ cup

variation:

Here's a little relish topper that works wonders on simply grilled tuna, salmon, or chicken: In a small bowl, combine ¹/₂ cup gremolata (above) with ¹/₃ cup chopped pitted Kalamata olives, 1 finely chopped stalk of celery, 1 tablespoon olive oil, ¹/₂ teaspoon dried oregano, and a squeeze of fresh lemon juice. Makes about ³/₄ cup.

buttermilk pie

This creamy, custardlike pie is an old favorite well worth revisiting. It's very easy to make and while the filling is quite rich, the end result is light, silky, and pleasantly tart. Serve the pie warm from the oven, or at room temperature. Sliced fresh fruit or berries make a lovely accompaniment. Refrigerate any leftovers.

Pastry for one unbaked **9**-inch pie shell

1 cup Lemon Sugar (page 49)

3 tablespoons flour

3 eggs, well beaten

½ cup (**1** stick) unsalted butter, melted and cooled slightly

1 cup buttermilk

2 tablespoons fresh lemon juice

2 teaspoons grated or finely chopped lemon zest

½ teaspoon pure vanilla extract

Preheat the oven to 425°F. Line a 9-inch pie pan with the pastry dough and prick with a fork. Line the shell with aluminum foil, pressing lightly to carefully fit the foil into the contours of the shell. Bake for 5 minutes. Remove the foil and bake for 4 or 5 minutes longer, until the edges of the crust just begin to color. Remove from the oven and set aside to cool completely.

Combine the lemon sugar and flour in a large mixing bowl. Add the beaten eggs and mix well. Stir in the melted butter, buttermilk, lemon juice and zest, and vanilla and pour into the pie shell. Place the pie in the center of the oven and bake for 15 minutes. Lower the heat to 350°F and bake for another 25 to 30 minutes, or until the filling is barely set.

Yield: one 9-inch pie

Note: If you don't have lemon sugar, regular sugar will work fine. Just increase the lemon juice to 3 tablespoons and the zest to 1 tablespoon.

strawberry-*lemon* pops

**Make these frozen treats when strawberries are at their peak of freshness.
They're a healthy alternative to their store-bought counterparts.**

2 cups (**1** pint) strawberries

2 tablespoons frozen lemonade concentrate

3 tablespoons sugar, or to taste

About **6** popsicle sticks

Wash and hull the strawberries. In a blender or food processor, puree the strawberries with the lemonade concentrate and sugar. Pour into disposable plastic cups, add sticks, and freeze until firm. Dip cups in warm water to loosen pops.

Yield: about 6 pops

lemon **ducks**

Use these whimsical waddlers as the centerpiece for an Easter luncheon or a child's birthday party. If you're not into ducks, use whatever cookie cutter shape pleases you. Mini cutters and aspic or canapé cutters produce bite-sized jewels perfect for garnishing a fruit plate or stacking in a stemmed glass.

Four **1**-ounce envelopes unflavored gelatin
¾ cup freshly squeezed lemon juice
¾ cup sugar
1 teaspoon grated or finely chopped lemon zest
1 to **2** drops yellow food coloring (optional)

Place 1 cup cold water in a medium bowl. Sprinkle the gelatin over the water and let stand for a few minutes.

Meanwhile, in a small saucepan, combine 3 cups water, the lemon juice, and sugar and heat until just boiling. Remove the pan from the heat and stir in the lemon zest. Pour the hot mixture over the water-and-gelatin mixture. Stir until the gelatin is dissolved, about 5 minutes. Stir in the food coloring, if using.

Pour into a 13-by-9-by-2-inch baking pan and refrigerate until firm, about 3 hours or up to overnight.

Press cookie cutters into the congealed gelatin to cut out shapes. Use a spatula to lift the shapes out of the pan and place them on a baking sheet or large platter. Cut leftover scraps into bite-sized free-form shapes for snacking. Cover and refrigerate ducks until ready to serve.

Yield: about eighteen 3-inch ducks

citrus suckers

Lollipops are lovely when they're made simply. In this recipe, a small, free-form puddle of lemony sugar syrup is garnished with a few bits of candied lemon peel and finished with a stick. If you want more uniform lollipops, you can use lollipop molds, which come in a variety of shapes and sizes.

Vegetable oil, for brushing
2 cups sugar
1 cup light corn syrup
Juice and grated or finely chopped zest of **1** large lemon
2 drops yellow food coloring (optional)
Short strips of candied lemon peel (optional)
About **15** lollipop sticks

Cover 2 baking sheets with waxed paper. Lightly brush the waxed paper with vegetable oil.

Combine the sugar with 1 cup water in a heavy saucepan. Add the corn syrup and cook over medium heat, stirring, just until the sugar dissolves. Bring mixture to a boil. Insert a candy thermometer and boil without stirring until the temperature reaches 280°F. Add the lemon juice and food coloring, if using, and cook over moderately high heat until the syrup reaches 300°F. Remove the pan from the heat and set briefly in a bowl of cool water to stop the cooking.

Once the bubbling subsides, stir in the lemon zest. Carefully spoon the mixture onto the prepared baking sheets in little puddles, about 2 inches in diameter. Working quickly, press a lollipop stick into each pop and decorate with the strips of candied lemon peel, if using. Cool for 30 minutes.

Yield: about 15 lollipops

Note: For gift giving, wrap each lollipop in clear cellophane or slip a cellophane lollipop bag (available at craft stores) over the top and tie with cord or ribbon. Arrange several sticks together in a short, pretty flower vase to make a lollipop bouquet.

lemon **sponge pudding**

This crowd-pleasing classic magically divides into two separate layers—creamy lemon pudding and light sponge cake—as it bakes. Serve warm or chilled, topped with a dollop of Lemon Whipped Cream or a scant dusting of confectioners' sugar and a few thin strands of lemon zest.

2 tablespoons unsalted butter, at room temperature, plus more for ramekins
⅔ cup sugar, plus more for ramekins
Pinch of salt
Grated zest of **1** large lemon
3 eggs, separated
3 tablespoons flour
¼ cup freshly squeezed lemon juice
¾ cup plus **1** tablespoon milk
Confectioners' sugar for dusting (optional)
Lemon Whipped Cream (recipe below)

Heat oven to 325°F. Butter four 6-ounce ramekins, individual ceramic pie pans, or glass custard cups. Coat with sugar. In a mixing bowl, combine the butter, sugar, and salt. Mix with an electric mixer on medium speed until crumbly. Mix in the lemon zest and egg yolks. Mix in the flour, then the lemon juice and milk.

In a separate bowl, beat the egg whites until stiff. Fold the beaten whites into the egg yolk mixture. Ladle into the prepared ramekins. Set the filled ramekins in a baking pan and pour hot water into the pan to come halfway up the sides of the ramekins. Bake for about 25 minutes, or until the puddings have set. Cool puddings on a wire rack for 20 minutes before serving. Serve in ramekins or invert onto plates and garnish.

Yield: 4 servings

lemon whipped cream

In a chilled, medium bowl, beat 1 cup chilled heavy cream with 2 tablespoons confectioners' sugar and 1 teaspoon *each* lemon juice and lemon zest until soft peaks form, about 2 minutes.

Yield: about 2 cups

lemon-**champagne sorbet**
garnished with frosted grapes

This impressive, make-ahead dessert is as easy to prepare as it is elegant. Any seedless grape will work, but tiny champagne grapes are especially lovely. Serve in chilled, stemmed glasses with a small cluster of grapes perched on one side.

for the sorbet:

1 cup sugar

⅓ cup freshly squeezed lemon juice

1 bottle (**750**ml) champagne or sparkling wine

2 teaspoons grenadine

for the frosted grapes:

1 pound seedless grapes, washed and patted dry

½ cup Lemon Sugar (page 49), or ½ cup regular sugar
    mixed with **1** teaspoon grated lemon zest

½ cup light corn syrup

To make the sorbet: Put the sugar in a nonreactive saucepan with 1 cup of water. Bring to a boil, stirring constantly until the sugar dissolves. Add the lemon juice, remove the syrup from the heat, and let cool. Refrigerate until cold. Combine the champagne and grenadine with the chilled syrup. Pour the mixture into an ice cream maker and freeze according to the manufacturer's instructions. Transfer the sorbet to a covered container and freeze overnight.

To make the frosted grapes: First divide the grapes into small clusters. Place the sugar in a small bowl. Holding each cluster by its stem, use a pastry brush to coat the grapes with the corn syrup, allowing any excess to drip off. Roll the cluster in the sugar and lemon zest mixture to coat. Transfer the sugar-frosted grapes to a parchment-lined baking sheet. Repeat with the remaining grape clusters and freeze until hard.

Yield: 8 to 10 servings

Note: The sorbet and the grapes can both be made up to 3 days ahead. Carefully transfer the frozen grapes to an airtight container and store in the freezer until ready to use.

lemon-**coconut cupcakes**

with *lemon*–cream cheese frosting

These pretty cupcakes are rich and dense but not too sweet. For a special gift, top each with a Honey Lemon Chip (page 52) and pack in a white bakery box decorated with lemon slice prints (page 103).

for the cupcakes:

1½ cups flour

½ teaspoon *each* baking powder and baking soda

Pinch of salt

¾ cup (1½ sticks) unsalted butter, at room temperature

1 cup sugar

3 large eggs, at room temperature

3 teaspoons grated or finely chopped lemon zest

½ teaspoon pure vanilla extract

½ cup sour cream

½ cup sweetened, shredded coconut

for the frosting:

8 ounces cream cheese, at room temperature

¼ cup (½ stick) unsalted butter, at room temperature

2 teaspoons grated or finely chopped lemon zest

½ teaspoon *each* pure vanilla extract and freshly squeezed lemon juice

2¼ cups confectioners' sugar

½ cup sweetened, shredded coconut

To make the cupcakes: Preheat the oven to 350°F. Line a 12-cup muffin tin with paper liners. Sift together the flour, baking powder, baking soda, and salt into a medium bowl. In a large bowl, cream the butter and sugar with an electric mixer until light and fluffy. Add the eggs, one at a time, beating after each addition. Scrape down the bowl and mix in the lemon zest and vanilla. Alternately add the flour mixture and the sour cream to the batter, beginning and ending with the flour. Mix until just combined. Fold in the coconut.

continued …

Spoon the batter into the cupcake liners. Bake for 20 minutes, or until the tops begin to brown slightly. Remove from the oven and transfer the individual cupcakes from the muffin tin to a rack to cool.

To make the frosting: In a large bowl, using an electric mixer, blend together the cream cheese, butter, lemon zest, vanilla, and lemon juice. Add the confectioners' sugar and mix until smooth. Stir in all but about 2 tablespoons of the coconut. Spread a thick layer of the frosting on the cupcakes and sprinkle with the remaining coconut.

Yield: 12 cupcakes

Note: If you have leftover frosting, store it in the refrigerator for up to 3 weeks, or freeze indefinitely. Bring to room temperature and stir briefly before using.

lemon-**blueberry muffins**

The perfect brunch treat, these crunchy-topped muffins look splendid packed in a basket lined with a linen napkin. Add a crock of softened cream cheese mixed with lemon zest, a newspaper, and a tin of tea to make a memorable "good morning" gift .

2 cups flour

1 tablespoon baking powder

2½ teaspoons grated or finely chopped lemon zest

½ teaspoon salt

1½ cups fresh blueberries

½ cup (**1** stick) unsalted butter, at room temperature

⅔ cup sugar, plus **1** tablespoon

2 eggs

1 tablespoon freshly squeezed lemon juice

1 teaspoon vanilla extract

¾ cup milk

1 teaspoon cinnamon

Preheat the oven to 350°F. Lightly grease a 12-cup nonstick muffin tin, or line with paper liners. In a medium bowl, combine the flour, baking powder, 2 teaspoons of the lemon zest, and salt. Stir to mix. Remove ¼ cup of the flour mixture and toss in a small bowl with the blueberries to coat. Set aside.

In a large bowl, cream the butter and the ⅔ cup sugar. Add the eggs, lemon juice, and vanilla and beat until smooth. Add the milk and mix well. Add the flour mixture and stir just until the dry ingredients are moistened. Do not overmix. Gently fold in the blueberries. Fill the muffin cups to the top with the batter. Combine the 1 tablespoon sugar, cinnamon, and remaining ½ teaspoon lemon zest and sprinkle over the tops. Bake for 20 to 25 minutes. Let the muffins sit for a few moments before removing them from the tin and placing on a wire rack. Serve warm or cooled.

Yield: 12 muffins

sherbet sandwiches

Lemon sherbet, sandwiched between crisp lemony cookies with just a hint of ginger, tastes like a breath of summertime. Paper-thin toasted almond slices add a crunchy texture to the outer edges of the sandwiches, but you can omit them if you like.

1¼ cups Lemon Sugar (page 49), or 1¼ cups regular
   sugar mixed with the grated zest of **2** lemons
2 cups flour
2 teaspoons baking powder
½ teaspoon baking soda
½ teaspoon ground ginger
Pinch of salt
½ cup (**1** stick) unsalted butter, at room temperature
1 large egg
2 teaspoons pure maple syrup
1 tablespoon freshly squeezed lemon juice
1 cup sliced almonds, lightly toasted (optional)
½ gallon lemon sherbet or sorbet, slightly softened

Place a rack in the upper third of the oven and preheat to 375°F. Line two baking sheets with parchment. Set aside ¼ cup of the lemon sugar. In a medium bowl, stir together the flour, baking powder, baking soda, ginger, and salt. In a large bowl, using an electric mixer, cream together the remaining cup of lemon sugar and the butter until light and fluffy. Add the egg, maple syrup, and lemon juice and beat until thoroughly blended. Gradually beat in the dry ingredients.

continued ...

Roll the dough into generous 1-inch balls and place on the prepared baking sheets, spacing them about 2 inches apart. Pour the reserved $\frac{1}{4}$ cup lemon sugar onto a small plate. Lightly grease the bottom of a glass. Flatten each cookie by first dipping the glass bottom into the lemon sugar and then pressing it on a ball. Bake for 8 to 10 minutes, until golden, with slightly darker edges. Let the cookies cool on the baking sheet for a minute or two before transferring them to racks to cool completely.

Spread the toasted, sliced almonds out on a plate, if using. Sandwich a generous scoop of sherbet between 2 cookies. Press the cookies together lightly and smooth the edges with a spatula. Roll the outer edges of the sandwich in sliced almonds to coat, if desired. If the sherbet gets too soft before you finish all the sandwiches, return it to the freezer for 15 to 20 minutes before continuing. Wrap each sandwich in plastic wrap and store in the freezer.

Yield: 10 to 15 sandwiches

lemon **curd**

Renowned for its starring role at English teas and in classic lemon tarts, this tangy, rich cream has an addictive quality—particularly when slathered on muffins, waffles, warm gingerbread, or biscuits. It also makes a wonderful filling for coconut cake, cookies, or meringues.

½ cup (**1** stick) unsalted butter, melted
1 cup sugar
½ cup freshly squeezed lemon juice, strained
2 tablespoons freshly grated lemon zest
Generous pinch of salt
6 egg yolks

Whisk together the melted butter, sugar, lemon juice, lemon zest, and salt in a medium, heavy-bottomed saucepan. Add the egg yolks and whisk until smooth.

Place the saucepan over low heat and cook slowly, stirring constantly with a wooden spoon, until the mixture thickens enough to coat the back of the spoon. Cook a minute or two longer, but do not allow the mixture to boil.

Remove from the heat. If desired, pour into small, dry, sterilized jars. Seal and allow to cool at room temperature, then refrigerate. If presenting as a gift, attach a tag that says "Refrigerate" and lists the use-by date. If not storing in jars, let the curd cool to room temperature in the saucepan, stirring occasionally. Use immediately or transfer to a covered container and refrigerate until ready to use. Lemon curd will keep in the refrigerator for 3 weeks and can be frozen for up to 2 months.

Yield: about 2 cups

Note: For a delightful hostess gift, fill a pretty jar with lemon curd and cover the lid with a pleated square of brown parchment or clip art of vintage lemon botanicals, tied with airy chiffon ribbon. Present the jar with Lemon-Blueberry Muffins (page 77) or a half dozen pre-baked individual tart shells packed into a Shaker-style box and tied with matching ribbon.

meyer *lemon* marmalade

Meyer lemons are smaller and have thinner skins than regular lemons and are not as sour (see page 21). If you don't live in an area where they are grown locally, look for them in specialty food shops. If you use regular lemons for this marmalade, substitute tangerines for half. The preserved marmalade will keep, stored in a cool, dark place, for up to a year. If using within a week or so, you can skip the water-bath process and store the marmalade in the refrigerator.

8 Meyer lemons
5 cups sugar

With a stiff brush, scrub the lemons under cold running water. Using a very sharp knife, slice the lemons into paper-thin slices. Remove the seeds and cut the slices into quarters. Place the lemon pieces in a large, nonreactive stockpot or copper jam pot and cover with 6 cups water. Cover the pot with plastic wrap and let sit at room temperature overnight.

Bring the lemon mixture to a boil. Lower the heat and simmer, uncovered, for 1 hour, or until the mixture is reduced to about 6 cups. Stir in the sugar and boil over moderate heat, stirring occasionally and skimming off any foam, until a teaspoon of the mixture dropped on a cold plate gels, about 30 to 40 minutes.

Ladle the hot marmalade into sterilized jars, leaving $1/4$ inch of headspace. Wipe the rims with a dampened cloth and seal. Process in a boiling water bath for 5 minutes (for half-pint or smaller jars) or according to the manufacturer's instructions.

Yield: about 4 pints

Note: Package a batch of this sunny spread in 4-ounce jars to save for holiday gift giving. Many small canning jars—particularly some of the European varieties—are so unique and attractive that they need nothing more than a festive tag or felt cutout for decoration.

the household *lemon*

Aside from being a culinary staple, the lemon has long been cele-
brated for its many practical uses. This final chapter offers ideas
for putting lemons to work around the house, as well as using them
to pamper the body and soul. In the following pages, you'll find
recipes for everything from a variety of natural cleaners to a luxurious collection of lotions and potions.

lemon-**lavender splash**

Since you won't be drinking the vodka used in this recipe, there is no need to reach for the top shelf. This recipe calls for fresh herbs. If you use dried herbs, use half the amount listed. Check laboratory and pharmacy supply stores for interesting glass containers or apothecary-style jars for storing this cologne. Or, make party favors for your next girls-only get-together by filling miniature antique perfume bottles with the splash and slipping the bottles into tiny organdy drawstring pouches from a craft store. See photograph, page 89.

Peel of **2** lemons
1 pint (**2** cups) vodka
2 cups orange flower water
¾ cup lavender
¾ cup lemon balm
¼ cup rosemary

Using a sharp knife, or a swivel-blade vegetable peeler, remove the zest of 2 lemons (without removing the white pith). Set lemons aside for another use. Combine zest with remaining ingredients in a large glass jar. Cover the jar and let steep for about a week. Strain the mixture and decant into a sterilized bottle. As long as the bottle is tightly covered and kept away from heat, the splash will keep indefinitely.

Yield: about 4 cups

lemon **lip balm**

Package this lip saver in fancy pill boxes, tiny tins, or recycled cosmetic containers. Make a fruity selection for a friend by filling the cups of an empty watercolor paint set with differently flavored lip balms. Choose a child's paint set with a clear plastic lid. Use a different fruit-scented essential oil to make a variety of balms. If you wish to tint the balms in colors that match the fragrance, use a toothpick to stir in a tiny bit of food coloring paste when you add the oil. Press little fruit stickers on the paint box lid over their corresponding balms.

1 tablespoon shea butter
½ teaspoon grated natural beeswax
Small, shallow tin can
Small skillet
5 drops lemon essential oil

Place the shea butter and beeswax in the can. Fill the skillet halfway with water to make a mini double boiler and place the can in the water. Bring the water to a boil. Heat until the shea butter and beeswax liquefy, being careful that no water gets into the mixture. Remove from the heat and stir in the lemon oil. Pour the mixture into small containers (see recipe introduction). Let cool and solidify before using.

Yield: about 1 tablespoon

Note: Shea butter is a natural, moisturizing fat and can be found at health food, vitamin supply, and natural product specialty stores.

lemon-lime layered bath oil

A bottle of this pousse café–style bath oil makes a lovely addition to any vanity shelf. The mixture separates into a translucent top layer with a pale chartreuse bottom layer. To package, replace the corks on vintage bottles or use clear dessert wine (half) bottles or olive oil bottles with the labels removed. Wrap the neck of the bottles with natural raffia or country twine with a handmade label tied to the end.

1 scant drop *each* yellow and green liquid food coloring
1 cup distilled water
Peel of ½ lemon, cut with a zester into a long spiraled strip
4 drops lemon essential oil
2 drops lime essential oil
⅔ cup almond oil

In a measuring cup, mix the food coloring with the water. Pour into a decorative bottle. Drop in the lemon peel. In a small bowl, combine the lemon and lime fragrances with the almond oil. Pour into the bottle on top of the water. In a few moments, the mixture will separate into two distinct layers. Shake well before using.

Yield: About 1⅔ cups

variation: *lemon*-ginger bath oil

No layers. Just silky, soothing loveliness. Mix 1 cup castor oil with 5 drops lemon essential oil and 3 drops ginger essential oil. Use 1 to 2 tablespoons per bath. Makes about 1 cup.

Right: Lemon-Lime Layered Bath Oil ›
Left: Lemon-Lavender Splash, recipe page 86.

lemon-mint foot bath

This refreshing potion is a luxurious way to pamper yourself. Use a large, white enamel basin or similar vessel that is pleasing to look at and large enough to accommodate your feet. (Yes, a dishpan will do, but this is a luxurious, at-home spa treatment so visuals count—you don't want to be thinking about dirty dishes while you do this!) Save the spent lemon halves—while your feet soak, rub the lemon halves over your elbows to relieve rough, dry patches.

3 cr **4** handfuls of smooth river stones
2 lemons
4 or **5** sprigs of fresh mint
A few drops of peppermint essential oil

Line the bottom of the basin with the stones and fill halfway with warm water. Slice one of the lemons in half and squeeze the juice into the water. Cut the other lemon into thin slices and drop into the water, along with the sprigs of mint. Add a splash of peppermint oil and insert feet. Soak for at least 10 minutes, massaging the feet by grabbing and releasing the stones with your toes.

cold-remedy trio

Colds sap your energy and dampen your spirits. These three lemony remedies may not cure the common cold, but they are delightful restoratives that will certainly make any cold-sufferer feel a bit better.

spicy *lemon*-ginger chicken broth

When you want the comfort of homemade broth, but don't have the time or energy to make it, reducing canned broth and spiking it with fresh herbs and lemon juice makes a good substitute. Be sure to use reduced-sodium broth, as regular canned chicken broth becomes much too salty when it is cooked down.

2 fresh chili peppers, such as serrano or jalapeño

2 stalks fresh lemongrass, trimmed of root ends
and grassy tops and sliced into **2**-inch pieces

One **1**-inch piece unpeeled fresh ginger, sliced

2 cloves unpeeled garlic

Two **14**-ounce cans reduced-salt chicken
broth, defatted

½ cinnamon stick

2 or **3** tablespoons fresh lemon juice, plus slices
for garnishing

Small bunch of fresh cilantro

Trim the stems from the chilies and cut in half lengthwise. With the flat edge of a large knife, smash the chilies, lemongrass, unpeeled ginger, and garlic. Place in a large saucepan and add the stock and cinnamon piece. Bring to a boil and cook for about 5 minutes to intensify the flavors. Lower the heat and simmer for 10 minutes. Strain the liquid into a bowl; return to the same pot. Discard the solids in the strainer. Return the broth to a simmer and stir in the lemon juice, tasting and adjusting the amount to your preference. Pour into mugs and garnish with a lemon slice and the fresh cilantro.

Yield: 4 servings

lemon cough syrup

In a jar, combine 1 cup honey and 3 tablespoons freshly squeezed lemon juice with ¼ cup hot water. Let cool and store, tightly covered, in the refrigerator. Use 1 to 2 teaspoons, as needed for cough.

Yield: about 1½ cups

lemon-and-peppermint sore throat remedy

For a simple soothing treat for a sore throat, roll a lemon on the counter to get the juices flowing, cut a hole in one end, and insert a peppermint-stick "straw." Old-fashioned, pure cane sugar peppermint sticks (the softer variety) work best. As the lemon juice is sucked up through the tiny pores in the stick, it begins to melt the candy, making the holes that the juice flows through larger. Replace the straw often.

lemon **meringue pie lotion**

This luxurious cream nourishes and softens dry skin, and has the scent and consistency of lemon pie filling. The key to making this lotion is to add the water and borax mixture to the oil and wax mixture very slowly (about ½ teaspoon at a time) to avoid separation, and to whisk constantly while combining. While not essential, an immersion blender or a small, handheld battery-operated whisk comes in handy for this task.

½ cup almond oil
¼ cup grapeseed oil
½ teaspoon lemon essential oil
¼ cup grated natural beeswax
¼ cup liquid glycerine
¼ cup distilled water
2 teaspoons borax

In a heavy-bottomed saucepan, combine all the oils with the beeswax and warm over low heat until the wax dissolves. Stir in the glycerine and keep at a low simmer while assembling the other mixture. (It is important that the two mixtures are the same temperature when you combine them.)

In a small pan, boil the water and add the borax, stirring until dissolved. Remove the two pans from the heat and very slowly pour the water and borax mixture into the oil mixture, whisking constantly until the mixture cools and forms a thick, opaque cream. Transfer the lotion to a pretty jar.

Yield: about 1 cup

little *lemon* soaps
in *lemon* leaf purses

For handmade elegance with minimal effort, make these lovely scented soaps with widely available melt-and-mold glycerine blocks. Craft stores offer a huge variety of soap molds, but a quick spin through the kitchen will produce suitable substitutes. Small tomato paste or 8-ounce pineapple cans, small milk cartons cut down to a 3-inch height, plastic ice cube trays, flexible candy molds, and rubber nonstick loaf pans and muffin pans all work well. If using cans for molds, select smooth-sided cans and coat them lightly with a little petroleum jelly before pouring in the glycerine. To unmold, simply remove the other end of the can and push the soap out. For milk cartons and rubber, plastic, or other flexible molds, you can skip the petroleum jelly step.

When you lay out guest towels for a weekend visitor, set a lemon leaf purse filled with miniature cubes of soap on top of the stack.

Sharp knife
10-ounce block unscented glycerine
2 drops yellow food coloring
20 drops lemon essential oil
Mini ice cube tray
8 to **12** large fresh lemon leaves of similar shape and size
Needle threaded with metallic gold or silver thread, or all-purpose tacky craft glue

With the sharp knife, cut the glycerine into small chunks. Place the chunks in a heavy-bottomed saucepan and heat over a very low flame until melted. (Alternatively, heat in a glass bowl in a microwave on low for 30-second intervals until melted.) Remove from the heat and stir in the food coloring and then the essential oil, adding more or less, as preferred. Pour the mixture into the mini ice cube tray and let sit at least 2 hours before unmolding. To unmold, simply flex the mold as you would with ice.

To make a purse, select two lemon leaves that are approximately the same size. With the front sides of the leaves facing outward, line up the edges and stitch or glue one long, curved edge together, leaving the top edge free. (If sewing, make small stitches on the outside. The metallic stitches add a charming, homespun look. If gluing, run the glue along the inside of the leaves, so it doesn't show.) Squeeze the unattached side of the purse open (like a change purse) and insert 3 to 5 mini soaps.

variations:

cubes of color

Embed the mini soap cubes in a large bar of a contrasting color and scent to make tutti-frutti soaps like the ones sold in fancy gift shops. Pour a second batch of the lemon base soap into a single large mold and let it cool slightly. Before it begins to harden, scatter in a handful of mini cubes. An opaque white base (see Lemon Creamsicles, page 99) filled with multicolored cubes also makes an exciting bar.

citrus scrubber

Cut a piece of loofah to the shape of your mold and place it in the bottom of the mold before pouring in the lemon soap mixture. The result is a unique combo of refreshing, astringent soap and exfoliating loofah all in one bar.

continued ...

citrus stripes

To make striped soaps, simply pour different layers of scented, tinted glycerine into a loaf pan, letting each layer harden before adding the next. For a major citrus hit, try a three-layered soap made up of a bottom orange stripe scented with tangerine oil, a middle stripe of yellow scented with lemon, and a top stripe of green with a lime scent. For gift giving, unmold the loaf and cut the soap into thick slabs. Wrap a strip of corrugated paper, rice paper, or natural burlap around each slice and tie with raffia or colored cord. Use an opaque marker to write the name of the soap on a citrus leaf and tuck it under the raffia.

additives and textures

Since glycerine is transparent, it is fun to add little visual pleasures to your soap. Cut a long strand of lemon zest and shape it into a spiral in the center of a round soap. Embed a small, plastic toy, such as a frog, in a bar. Sprinkle oatmeal, cornmeal, or poppy seeds into soap to create an interesting texture as well as a gentle exfoliant. For a spicy-citrus scent, add whole cloves to a lemon soap. Use a flexible rubber muffin pan to make an exciting soap selection by adding a different textural element, color, and scent to each cup. Keep in mind that perishable additives will give your soaps a shorter shelf life, so they should be used shortly after they are prepared.

lemon creamsicle

Make the basic lemon soap as described above, but pour it into a loaf pan rather than an ice cube tray. Let harden. Melt another 10 ounces of glycerine and remove from the heat when it has liquefied. Stir in $\frac{1}{2}$ cup heavy cream and 20 drops vanilla essential oil. Pour the cream mixture on top of the first layer and let harden. The result will be a yellow, transparent lemon layer and a white, opaque vanilla layer. Slice the soap into bars. Wrap the bars in pale glassine or baker's parchment tied up with ribbon embroidery silk or hemp cord and a whole vanilla bean.

beauty box

An array of pampering lemon luxuries makes a great gift for a busy friend. Fill a galvanized or nylon mesh storage cube, a small galvanized washtub, or a large, shallow white porcelain or enamel bowl with crisp white hand towels, rolled and tied with pale yellow satin ribbon. Add a wedge of Lemon Creamsicle Soap (page 99), a tin of Lemon Lip Balm (page 87), and bottles of Lemon-Lavender Splash (page 86), Lemon Meringue Pie Lotion (page 94), and Lemon-Ginger Bath Oil (page 88). Top with a fresh lemon branch with fruits attached or a small bouquet of lemon herbs. Any of the following quickie concoctions would also make a lovely addition to the box.

lemon bath salts

Combine ½ cup sea salt or coarse kosher salt, ⅓ cup borax, ¼ cup baking soda, 10 drops lemon essential oil, and 4 drops liquid yellow food coloring. Stir well to distribute the food coloring and crush any lumps with the back of the spoon. When the mixture turns pale yellow and is lump-free, spread it out on a dinner plate and let dry overnight. (The room that it dries out in will be beautifully perfumed the next morning.) Package the bath salts in hand-decorated pastel envelopes.

Yield: about 1 cup

lemon bath powder

Combine 1 cup cornstarch with 15 to 20 drops of lemon essential oil. Crush any lumps with the back of a spoon. Package the powder in a glass sugar or cheese shaker that has large holes in the top.

Yield: 1 cup

fizzy *lemon* bath cubes

Heat ½ cup shea butter in a microwave on low for 30-second intervals until it liquefies. (Or use a double boiler.) Remove from the heat and stir in ½ cup baking soda, ¼ cup citric acid, and 6 tablespoons cornmeal. Add about 10 drops lemon essential oil and stir well. Spoon the mixture into an ice cube tray and let sit for about an hour until the cubes harden. Unmold and wrap the cubes in precut squares of colored foil from a confectionery supply store.

Yield: 10 to 12 cubes

bay-*lemon* liquid hand soap

Bring 2 cups water to a boil. Add 1 tablespoon unscented glycerine soap and stir until it dissolves. Remove from the heat and add 8 drops lemon essential oil and 6 drops West Indian bay essential oil. Cool and pour into a decorative pump bottle.

Yield: about 2 cups

house-cleaning quartet

Lemons have myriad practical uses. These simple homemade products leave a fresh scent on furniture and in the air.

air freshener

In a spray bottle, combine 1 part liquid glycerine with 4 parts water. Add drops of lemon essential oil until the desired scent intensity is acquired. Shake before spraying. After a few weeks, you may wish to add additional drops of lemon oil, as the scent will weaken as the liquid begins to evaporate.

stain remover

Mix together equal parts lemon juice and cream of tartar to make a spot bleach for stained whites. Dab the mixture on the spot and leave for a few minutes. Blot with a wet sponge. This works for most household stains and even some types of rust.

furniture polish

In a tightly covered jar, shake together 1 cup linseed oil and $^3/_4$ cup malt vinegar. Add 1 teaspoon lemon essential oil and shake again. To dust furniture, shake well and pour a small amount onto a soft cotton cloth. Wipe surface with the cloth, then buff off any excess with a clean, dry cloth.

Yield: about 1$^3/_4$ cups

surface cleaner

Combine 2 cups warm water, $^3/_4$ cup lemon juice, $^1/_2$ cup baking soda, and a few drops of lemon essential oil. Pour into a spray bottle and use to clean surfaces that you would normally clean with commercial ammonia-based cleaners.

Yield: about 2$^3/_4$ cups

lemon **print note cards**

These printed note cards couldn't be easier to make, and a packet of them makes a wonderful gift. Wrap a stack of cards, with matching envelopes, in a piece of transparent vellum or tracing paper and tie with a pastel chiffon ribbon. Tuck a couple of fresh lemon leaves under the bow. Lemon prints can also be used to decorate gift wrap, shopping bags, paper boxes, or place cards.

2 or **3** lemons
Paper towels
Scrap paper
Yellow liquid acrylic craft paint
White (for a subtle effect) or brightly colored (for high impact) blank cards
    with matching envelopes

To make a lemon printer, cut a lemon in half and blot it on a paper towel to remove excess juice. Pour a small puddle of paint onto a flat-bottomed plate. Dip the cut side of the lemon into the paint and swirl it around to make sure the entire surface is covered. Blot it lightly on the paper towel, then press it firmly onto a piece of scrap paper, making sure it doesn't slip around. Experiment with the scrap paper until you are happy with the lemon slice print you are getting. (Some lemons make better printers than others, so you may need to slice one or two until you find the perfect one.) Once you are satisfied with your lemon printer, proceed with the cards, making a single print on the front of each. Let dry for at least 30 minutes before using.

little *lemon* cachepot

Here, a lemon half makes a fragrant container for a miniature floral arrangement. Place one of these charming cachepots next to each place setting for a special dinner party, or use one to brighten an overnight guest's bedside table. Be sure to use freshly cut, sturdy-stemmed herbs and greenery, and make herb cachepots the day you plan to use them.

Lemons (**1** lemon makes **2** cachepots)

For a summer herb arrangement: short (**2**- to **3**-inch) sprigs of herbs such as rosemary, lavender, and sage

For a winter greenery arrangement: short (**2**- to **3**-inch) sprigs of assorted evergreens

Slice a lemon in half lengthwise. Push the stems of the sprigs into the lemon pulp. The pulp works like florist's foam to hold the stems in place. As long as all your stems are nice and sturdy, they will push right in. If one needs a little help, punch a small hole into the pulp with a toothpick and then insert the sprig. Make a pleasing arrangement, covering the entire surface of the pulp with sprigs. If using at the table, you may wish to tuck a placecard into each arrangement.

berry variation:

To add a spot of contrasting color to your cachepots, add fresh blueberries or cranberries to your arrangements. Push a berry onto the end of a toothpick. Push the toothpick into the lemon, nestling it among the greenery so the toothpick doesn't show (break the toothpick if you need it to be shorter).

pomanders

Lemon pomanders are lovely piled in a pretty bowl. Tie a ribbon around a pomander and hang it in your closet, or tie it to the top of a wrapped package. During the holidays, adorn the mantelpiece with pine boughs, fat beeswax candles, pomanders, carved lemons, and Sugared Lemons (page 108).

6 large lemons
About ½ cup whole cloves
Wooden skewer
Citrus zester or channel knife

Punch method: With a wooden skewer, punch a hole in a lemon about ⅛ inch deep. Push the long end of a clove into the hole, leaving the bud exposed. Continue until the entire lemon is randomly covered with cloves spaced about ⅜ inch apart. Or, punch holes in rows to create stripes or a simple design, leaving areas of the lemon uncovered.

Carve method: Use a zester to cut decorative canals into the lemon peel, revealing the soft white pith beneath. With this method, the cloves can be pushed right into the canal pattern you have cut out. There is no need to punch a hole with a skewer. For a simple spiral design, start at the top of a lemon, moving slowly and keeping the zester pressed firmly against the lemon, and cut around and around until you reach the other end. Push cloves into the spiral canal, spacing them evenly apart. Experiment with other designs, such as vertical stripes and free-form zigzags.

Yield: 6 pomanders

Note: The instant gratification of this particular craft makes it hard to stop once you get started. For this reason, you may wish to buy extra lemons and cloves. If you are making a large arrangement, include oranges and limes for variety. It's also fun to mix in some fruits that are just carved, but have no cloves inserted.

If you are making pomanders for hanging, use the zester to carve a canal path for a thin piece of ribbon or cord to fit into so that it doesn't slip around when you tie it around the lemon.

sugared *lemons*

While their frosty appearance makes sugared lemons a natural for winter holiday decorating, they are stunning any time of year. Nestle a few into a live wheat grass arrangement or a clear glass bowl lined with lemon leaves. Use single sugared lemons, tied around the middle with a shimmering piece of ribbon and a fresh herb sprig, as place markers for a special dinner party.

4 egg whites
Wooden skewer
6 lemons
Pastry brush or **1**-inch paintbrush
About **1** cup regular sugar or coarse sanding sugar

Classic method: Combine the egg whites with a few drops of water and beat with a fork until frothy. Insert the skewer into the end of a lemon. Over a protected surface, hold the lemon by the skewer "handle" and use the pastry brush or paintbrush to paint the lemon with the egg white mixture, covering the entire surface. Sprinkle the sugar over the lemon with a spoon, holding the lemon over a bowl to catch the granules that do not adhere. Set the lemon on a piece of waxed paper to dry. Repeat the process with the other lemons. Or, instead of covering the entire lemon with sugar, dip a small craft paintbrush into the egg whites to paint simple designs—such as stripes, plaids, swirls, or dots— on the lemon. The sprinkled sugar will adhere to the design only, making a subtle pattern.

Quickie method: As long as you never intend to eat the lemons, you can substitute spray adhesive (from a craft or art supply store) for the egg whites. Just spray on to coat the lemon, then sprinkle on the sugar. This method will not only be quicker, but the finished lemons will be more stable and will hold up longer than those done with egg whites.

Yield: 6 sugared lemons

lemon **herb windowsill garden**

Fresh fruit is not the only source of lemony flavor and aroma. This trio of lemon-scented herbs thrives indoors on a sunny windowsill with a southern or western exposure and at least 4 good hours of sunlight every day. The herbs need to be turned or moved periodically so that they grow evenly as they reach toward the light source. This picket fence planter makes turning all three pots at once a snap. When you are ready to cook with the herbs, simply snip them fresh. The planter can also serve as a lovely, casual dinner table centerpiece.

Carpet tacks

About seventy-five (depending on the length of your windowsill) 6-inch wooden plant markers, rounded on one end and pointed on the other

Hammer

One 6-inch-wide, 1-inch-thick board, cut 1 inch shorter than the interior length of your windowsill

2-inch paintbrush

White latex paint

Three 4½-inch flower pots, with saucers, planted one each with lemon thyme, lemon-scented geranium, and lemon verbena (since they won't show, it is fine to use mismatched or lightweight plastic pots)

Using a single carpet tack for each wooden plant marker, nail the markers, side by side and pointy side up, around all four 1-inch edges of the board, forming a box shape, with the board becoming the bottom of the box. Be sure to keep the bottoms of the plant markers even with the bottom of the board.

Paint the picket fence box inside and out with the white paint. When the paint is dry, set the three potted herbs, along with their saucers, inside the box and place it in the windowsill.

Note: If you can't find wooden plant markers, use wooden tongue depressors, which are sold in bulk at craft stores. For a rustic, woodsy look, gather twigs and sticks to use instead of the plant markers. Cut them all to the same length before proceeding and omit the painting step. Depending on the diameter of the twigs, your finished windowbox may be an inch or so wider than those made with flat plant markers, so make sure your windowsill can accommodate the extra width.

cleansing candle

When lit, this candle releases the appealing scents of lemon and juniper to cleanse the air and add a fresh, natural scent. Its pale and slightly frosted appearance is created by cooling and gently beating the wax before pouring into the mold. Good craft stores stock an array of candle molds, but found containers such as waterproof cardboard or plastic food cartons can be used and simply torn away or removed and discarded once the candle has hardened. To decorate, tie with a wide piece of organdy ribbon and accent with a sprig of fresh juniper or lavender, a small lemon tree branch, or a sprig of pink pepperberries.

Quart-size empty milk carton, for mold

Permanent marker

1 pound yellow or green candle-making wax

Double boiler

One **8**-inch piece candlewick

Pencil

About **10** drops lemon essential oil and **6** drops juniper oil, or to preference

Small wire whisk

Cut just the top off the milk carton, leaving as much height as possible. You will be swirling the wax around it, so you need the extra height to prevent spillage. The finished candle will be 5 inches tall. Mark the height by drawing a line with the permanent marker on the outside of the carton 5 inches from the bottom. Pierce a small hole in the center of the bottom of the carton.

Cut the wax into small chunks and heat in the double boiler until melted. Remove from the heat. Dip all but about 3 inches of the wick into the melted wax and hold it there for a few seconds. Remove the wick, let cool for a few seconds, and then run your fingers down the length of it to straighten it. Thread the wick through the hole at the base of the carton, making sure that the unwaxed end is at the top of the carton. Leave about ¹/₂ inch of the waxed

continued ...

end outside the hole, flatten it against the carton bottom, and plug up the hole on the outside of the carton with a dab of soft wax. Make sure the wick is centered. Pull it taut and wrap the excess end of the wick around the pencil. Lay the pencil across the top of the carton.

If the wax in the double boiler has begun to harden, reheat it. Remove the wax from the heat and add the essential oils. Whisk the wax gently and constantly as it cools, watching the surface. When a little foam begins to form on the surface, pour about $\frac{1}{2}$ cup of the wax into the carton. Swish the wax around in the carton, coating the inside just up to the 5-inch mark. When the carton's interior is coated, pour the excess wax back into the pot, reheat if necessary, and whisk the wax again until it becomes foamy. Pour the foamy wax into the carton, filling it up to the mark. Reserve a generous tablespoonful of wax for topping off later.

Let sit for 5 minutes, then tap the mold to release any trapped air bubbles. As it cools, the candle will develop a slight indentation around the wick. Reheat the reserved wax and use it to top off the candle. Let cool and harden completely. Trim the bottom wick flush with the base of the candle. Remove the pencil and snip off the unwaxed portion of the top wick, leaving about an inch of wick exposed. Tear off the carton mold and discard.

lemon **potpourri**

When making potpourri, be sure that all the ingredients are perfectly dry so it won't develop mold. For a quick sachet, place a cupful of this mixture in the center of a clean handkerchief or linen napkin. Gather the edges of the cloth to form a pouch and tie at the neck with a pretty ribbon. Attach a single dried lemon slice.

2 cups lemon verbena
1 cup lemon balm
½ cup bay leaves
¼ cup rosemary
Zest of **2** lemons, dried
6 to **8** dried lemon slices (optional, see note)
Four **3**-inch cinnamon sticks, broken into small pieces
2 tablespoons whole cloves
6 to **8** drops lemon essential oil

Mix all the ingredients in a large glass bowl. For an intense and fully developed potpourri, store the mixture in a large covered container, in a cool dark place, for about 4 weeks, shaking every few days.

Yield: About 5 cups

variation: simmering *lemon* potpourri

Make a simmering citrus potpourri to perfume your home for the winter holidays. Fill a large saucepan with 4 cups water, the rind of 2 lemons and 1 orange, 6 sprigs of fresh rosemary, 6 cinnamon sticks, and a generous pinch of whole cloves. Bring to a boil, then allow to simmer, checking from time to time to replenish the water as it evaporates.

Note: Dried lemon slices can be purchased online from specialty purveyors or ordered through a florist. Drying lemon slices in your oven can sometimes render uneven results, but it's a simple process, and if you double the amount you need, you will probably end up with enough usable slices: Preheat the oven to the lowest setting (140°F is ideal). Slice lemons about ⅛ inch thick and lay them on a wire cake rack set on a baking sheet, making sure that no slices are touching. Dry with the oven door cracked, for 3 to 8 hours, checking periodically. The slices should be completely dried, leathery, and slightly curled at the edges, but not brown.

resources

Anthropologie
Stores nationwide.
(800) 543-1039
www.anthropologie.com
Housewares, kitchen accessories.

Aromatique
London, England
(020) 7591 1950
www.aromatique.com
Room fragrances, candles, essential oils.

Artistic Ribbon
New York, New York
(212) 255-4224
www.artisticribbon.com
Ribbons, trims, and cords.

Bell'occhio
San Francisco, California
(415) 864-4048
www.bellocchio.com
Ribbons, creative packaging.

Ben Franklin
Stores nationwide.
www.benfranklin.com
General art and craft supplies.

The Candlemaker
Greendale, Wisconsin
(888) 251-4618
www.thecandlemaker.com
Candle-making supplies.

The Container Store
Dallas, Texas
(214) 654-2000
www.containerstore.com
Creative packaging solutions.

Crate & Barrel
Stores nationwide.
(800) 967-6696
www.crateandbarrel.com
Baking and cooking supplies, housewares.

Dick Blick
Galesburg, Illinois
(800) 447-8192
www.dickblick.com
Candle-making supplies, general art supplies.

Divertimenti
London, England
(020) 7581 8065
www.divertimenti.co.uk
Kitchenware, baking supplies, tableware.

Earth Guild
Asheville, North Carolina
(800) 327-8448
www.earthguild.com
Candle-making supplies, including colored
wax; soap-making supplies, including
glycerine blocks.

Fantasy Fare
London, England
(020) 7916 2100
Craft materials, haberdashery.

Gardener's Supply Company
Burlington, Vermont
(800) 427-3363
www.gardeners.com
Wooden plant markers.

Grace Manufacturing
Russellville, Arkansas
(501) 968-5445
www.microplane.com
Microplane zester.

Hold Everything
Stores nationwide.
(800) 421-2264
www.holdeverything.com
Creative packaging solutions.

Hyman Hendler and Sons
New York, New York
(212) 840-8393
www.hymanhendler.com
New and vintage ribbons, trims, and cords.

John Lewis PLC
London, England
(020) 7629 7711
www.johnlewis.co.uk
Kitchenware, baking supplies, tableware.

Kate's Paperie
New York, New York
(888) 941-9169
www.katespaperie.com
Art papers, ribbon, creative packaging
solutions, blank note cards.

Katz & Company
Napa, California
(800) 676-7176
www.katzandco.com
Meyer lemons.

The King Arthur Flour Company
Norwich, Vermont
(800) 827-6836
www.bakerscatalogue.com
Silicone flexible muffin pans, candied lemon
peel, microplane zester, pure lemon oil.

Kitchen Krafts
Waukon, Iowa
(800) 776-0575
www.kitchenkrafts.com
Candy-making, baking, canning, and
cooking supplies.

The Lebermuth Co.
South Bend, Indiana
(800) 259-7000
www.lebermuth.com
Essential oils, herbs, spices.

M & J Trimming
New York, New York
(212) 391-9072
www.mjtrim.com
New and vintage ribbons, trims, and cords.

Michaels
Stores nationwide.
(800) 642-4235
www.michaels.com
General art and craft supplies.

Mountain Rose Herbs
Eugene, Oregon
(800) 879-3337
www.mountainroseherbs.com
Essential oils, bulk herbs, bulk cosmetic
ingredients, cosmetic containers.

Neal's Yard Remedies
London, England
(020) 7379 7222
www.nealsyardremedies.com
Herbal beauty products, homeopathic
remedies, essential oils.

New York Central Art Supply
New York, New York
(800) 950-6111
www.nycentralart.com
Unique papers, general art supplies
(swatches available).

L'Occitane
London, England
(020) 7290 1426
www.loccitane.net
Natural beauty products, balms, and
perfumes made from essential oils.

Pearl Paint
Stores nationwide.
(800) 451-7327
www.pearlpaint.com
General art and craft supplies.

Pottery Barn
Stores nationwide.
(888) 779-5176
www.potterybarn.com
Housewares, creative packaging solutions.

Pourette
Seattle, Washington
(800) 888-9425
www.pourette.com
Candle- and soap-making supplies.

Restoration Hardware
Stores nationwide.
(877) 747-4671
www.restorationhardware.com
Housewares, kitchen accessories, gardening supplies.

Savonnerie
Immaculate House
London, England
(020) 7375 1844
Natural soaps and bath oils, essential oils.

Soapcrafters
Salt Lake City, Utah
(801) 484-5121
www.soapcrafters.com
Soap-making supplies, lotion-making
supplies, containers.

Sur La Table
Stores nationwide.
(800) 243-0852
www.surlatable.com
Candy-making, baking, canning, and
cooking supplies.

Tinsel Trading Company
New York, New York
(212) 730-1030
www.tinseltrading.com
New and vintage ribbons, trims, and cords.

The Vermont Country Store
Manchester Center, Vermont
(802) 362-2400
www.vermontcountrystore.com
Old-fashioned porous peppermint sticks,
microplane zester, jars.

Williams-Sonoma
Stores nationwide.
(877) 812-6235
www.williams-sonoma.com
Baking and cooking supplies, housewares.

bibliography

Bacon, Josephine. "Search for the Sour and the Importance of the Citron." In *Oxford Symposium on Food and Cookery, Taste Proceedings,* edited by Tom Jaine. London: Prospect Books, 1988.

Bonavia, Emanuel. *Oranges and Lemons of India and Ceylon.* 1888. Reprint, Dehra Dun: Bishen Singh Mahendra Pal Singh and Periodical Experts, 1973.

Brenzel, Kathleen Norris, ed. *Sunset Western Garden Book,* 7th ed. Menlo Park, CA: Sunset Publishing, 2001.

Brothwell, Don, and Patricia Brothwell. *Food in Antiquity.* Baltimore: The Johns Hopkins University Press, 1998.

Corriher, Shirley. *Cookwise.* New York: William Morrow and Co., 1997.

Davidson, Alan. *Fruit.* New York: Simon and Schuster, 1991.

———. *The Oxford Companion to Food.* Oxford: Oxford University Press, 1999.

Field, Michael. *All Manner of Food.* New York: Ecco Press, 1982.

Hobhouse, Penelope. *Gardening Through the Ages.* New York: Simon and Schuster, 1992.

Jenner, Thomas. *The Book of Fruits and Flowers: Shewing the Nature and Use of Them, Either for Meat or Medicine.* 1656. Reprint, London: Prospect Books, 1984.

Morton, Julia F. *Fruits of Warm Climates.* Miami: JF Morton Publishing, 1987.

Perry, Charles. "Preserved Lemons." *Petits Propos Culinaire 50.* London: Prospect Books, 1995.

Romaine, Effie, and Sue Hawkey. *Herbal Remedies in Pots.* New York: DK Publishing, 1996.

Susser, Allen. *The Great Citrus Book.* Berkeley: Ten Speed Press, 1997.

Tannahill, Reay. *Food in History.* New York: Crown Trade Paperback, 1988.

Wilson, Anne C. *Food and Drink in Britain from the Stone Age to the 19th Century.* Chicago: Academy Chicago Publishers, 1991.

index

table of equivalents

The exact equivalents in the following tables have been rounded for convenience.

liquid and dry measures

u.s.	metric
¼ teaspoon	**1.25** milliliters
½ teaspoon	**2.5** milliliters
1 teaspoon	**5** milliliters
1 tablespoon (**3** teaspoons)	**15** milliliters
1 fluid ounce (**2** tablespoons)	**30** milliliters
¼ cup	**60** milliliters
⅓ cup	**80** milliliters
1 cup	**240** milliliters
1 pint (**2** cups)	**480** milliliters
1 quart (**4** cups, **32** ounces)	**960** milliliters
1 gallon (**4** quarts)	**3.84** liters
1 ounce (by weight)	**28** grams
1 pound	**454** grams
2.2 pounds	**1** kilogram

length measures

u.s.	metric
⅛ inch	**3** millimeters
¼ inch	**6** millimeters
½ inch	**12** millimeters
1 inch	**2.5** centimeters

oven temperatures

fahrenheit	celsius	gas
250	120	½
275	140	1
300	150	2
325	160	3
350	180	4
375	190	5
400	200	6
425	220	7
450	230	8
475	240	9
500	260	10